PRAISE FOR
swimming with scapulars

"[*Swimming with Scapulars*] shatters many stereotypes. If you have been wondering about the emergence of an informed and sophisticated group of orthodox young Catholics who take the spiritual life seriously, this book will reveal a fascinating group of people. . . . As someone who knows many people like this, I am encouraged that the church is beginning to regain its identity at the grass roots."

—Benedict J. Groeschel, CFR, author
of *The Reform of Renewal*

"This defense of the faith, from a married father of four who has clung unapologetically to it, will be food for many Catholic souls."

—*The San Diego Union-Tribune*

"As personal faith stories go, Lickona's is a breath of fresh air, thoughtfully written and happily absent of platitudes and pious moralizing. . . . Most readers . . . will find themselves captivated by this winsome story of a soul."

—*Publishers Weekly*

"This is a highly personal account of a young man seriously trying to live the Catholic faith in America today; it will encourage Catholics and entertain them. Lickona faces the difficulties and appreciates the blessing of belonging to Christ and the church in an often hostile and uncertain world, and he does so with literacy and style."

—Francis Cardinal George, OMI,
archbishop of Chicago

"*Swimming with Scapulars* is . . . a frank, thoughtful, funny first book that I hope won't be Lickona's last."

—*The Catholic Register*

swimming with scapulars

swimming with scapulars

TRUE CONFESSIONS OF A YOUNG CATHOLIC

matthew lickona

LOYOLAPRESS.

CHICAGO

LOYOLAPRESS.

3441 N. ASHLAND AVENUE
CHICAGO, ILLINOIS 60657
(800) 621-1008
WWW.LOYOLABOOKS.ORG

A substantial portion of the book appeared, in somewhat different form, in the *San Diego News Notes*.

All Scripture quotations are taken from the Revised Standard Version of the Bible, Catholic Edition, except for the quotation from Proverbs, which is taken from the Challoner-Douay Version.

Out of regard for privacy, some names have been changed.

Cover photograph by Georgia Kokolis/Getty Images
Author photograph by Sandy Huffaker Jr.

Jacket design by Adam Moroschan
Interior design by Laura Steur

Library of Congress Cataloging-in-Publication Data
Lickona, Matthew.
   Swimming with scapulars : true confessions of a young Catholic / Matthew Lickona.
        p. cm.
   ISBN-10: 0-8294-2072-X ISBN-13: 978-0-8294-2072-2
   1. Lickona, Matthew. 2. Catholics—United States—Biography. I. Title.
BX4705.L624A3 2005
282'.092—dc22
                                                           2004025209
First paperback printing, January 2007
paperback ISBN: 978-0-8294-2471-3

Printed in the United States of America
07 08 09 10 11 12 Versa 10 9 8 7 6 5 4 3 2 1

For Jim Holman and Judith Moore

contents

ᔕᔕᔕᔕᔕ

acknowledgments

௸ ௸ ௸ ௸ ௸

I WOULD LIKE TO THANK the following people in particular:

My mother and father, my first teachers in so many things, especially the life of faith and the habit of writing.

My wife, Deirdre, for patience and support and a swift kick when I need it.

My children, for being constant reminders of mercy and love.

Mark and Lisa Lickona, for love and theology.

Jim Manney and Joe Durepos at Loyola Press, for taking me on and helping to shape this book; and Erica Orloff, for her valuable comments.

Michael Horton, for good wine and good talk.

And finally, Our Lady of Perpetual Help, on whose feast I was born, in whose church I was married, and upon whose intercession I rely.

preface

&)&)&)&)&)

CHRISTMAS EVE OF 1992 found me just off the coast of Florida, getting pounded silly by the early morning waves. I was nineteen, and I enjoyed throwing myself against the six-footers as they broke. I enjoyed the roaring violence of it: the way my body's motion was suddenly halted and reversed; the way I was thrown down by the surrounding water, spun around, and held under so that I lost my sense of direction; the way I had to fight my way back above water, sometimes against a sucking riptide. But after one particularly disorienting collision, and a riptide that gripped me long enough to engender that moment of thrilling terror—*will I make it up?*—I gained the surface and found I had lost my scapular.

"Whosoever dies wearing this scapular shall not suffer eternal fire." Tradition holds this to be the promise given by the Blessed Virgin Mary upon the garment's presentation to the

Carmelite Prior St.-Simon Stock in 1251. Though I had been enrolled in the scapular—two small squares of brown wool connected by strings and worn around the neck—for the better part of a year, I didn't understand how it "worked." Surely an article of clothing could not guarantee salvation? The promise sounded almost dangerous, a temptation to presume upon God's mercy.

But then, I supposed, if you were not one of the elect, then God would see to it that you were not wearing your scapular at the time of your death. I imagined an adulterous husband, rushing home from an illicit interlude and losing control of his car on a rain-slick road. He slams into a tree, and as he sails through the windshield and heads for the pavement at seventy miles an hour, the last thing he sees is his scapular, dangling from a shard of broken glass. God is not mocked.

As I felt the bare patch of skin on my chest where the wool square used to be, I thought of my own soul, itself weighted with sin. Was God finished being merciful with me? Was He preparing to take my life and subject me to judgment, now that I was out from under Our Lady's promise? I panicked, and thrashed my way to shore.

What was I thinking, fighting riptides with serious sin— and the consequent threat of hell—on my soul? I once heard it said that if Christians really believed that Christ was in the tabernacle, they would never leave the church. Similarly, if I really believed my eternal fate was in jeopardy, why wasn't I curled up on a priest's doorstep, begging him to hear my confession?

I don't really have an answer, except to say that growing up with God and the devil, heaven and hell, Jesus and Mary, sin and salvation, and all the rest of it had made them familiar to me, perhaps too familiar. It was easy to overlook their significance, easy to ignore the urgency and import of their existence. At nineteen, death and what came after felt very far away. That last riptide, combined with my lost scapular, brought them a little bit nearer.

The years since then have served to wipe away still more of the tarnish brought on by familiarity, to allow me a clearer look at the tradition I have inherited. And even by Christmas of 1992, I was taking my spiritual life more seriously than I had just a few years before. Already, I had begun poking around amid the more ancient treasures of the faith, full of wonder (if not perfect understanding) at what I beheld. Already, I had become one of those people who go swimming with scapulars.

PART I

∽∽∽∽∽

FORMATION

∽∽∽∽∽

ᔥᔥᔥᔥᔥ

the janitor prophet

THE NIGHT MY WIFE, DEIRDRE, went into labor with our fourth child, we put the older three to bed, then settled in to watch *The Spy Who Came In from the Cold.* By film's end, the contractions were coming a little over five minutes apart. We replayed Richard Burton's final speech, the one that laid bare the moral loathing he felt for his own spy's-life amorality. We hashed out the machinations that had brought the film to its less-than-cheerful end. We kept timing the contractions. Around midnight, we called a friend to come sit with the kids and headed for the hospital.

Elijah Timothy Lickona was born into the San Diego night ninety minutes later—not as fast as Olivia, our third (seventy-five minutes from the time the contractions woke Deirdre from sleep), but much faster than our first two. Ninety minutes is not a long time as hard labor goes, but mind-blowing pain has a way of stretching time out, so it didn't feel all that short to Deirdre.

My wife has delivered all four of our children without medication. She does this for a number of reasons, not least of which is her belief in St. Paul's claim that "in my flesh I complete what is lacking in Christ's afflictions for the sake of his body, that is, the church" (Colossians 1:24). She offers the pain of her labor to God for the health of her baby and for her mother's return to the Catholic Church. The catch is that, when things get really bad—when the low growl she makes when bearing down through the contraction gives way to a wavering cry, endlessly rising in pitch and volume—she cannot pray. She cannot even think. When I look at Deirdre in these moments, her eyes squeezed shut and her tiny mouth wide open, it seems to me she is not there. My wife, my pillar of strength and stability, is lost in a miasma of pain.

So I pray for her—not for her relief, but on her behalf. I lean over her and speak in low tones at a steady clip, "Lord Jesus, accept this suffering as an offering for the salvation of Deirdre's mother, for her return to the church, and for the health of the baby. Lord, give her strength to bear this suffering." I try not to imagine what the attendant nurses must be thinking.

This woman is screaming in agony, and her husband, instead of offering comfort, instead of speaking words of worshipful praise about how great she is doing and how we're almost there and everything's going to be okay, is talking to God. He is not asking for deliverance, not asking the baby to be born sooner than later. He is asking for acceptance—easy for him to ask. What kind of coldhearted man is this? What kind of cold-hearted God is receiving his prayers? What kind of coldhearted religion would inspire such behavior?

◈◈◈◈◈

I AM A ROMAN CATHOLIC, baptized as an infant and raised in the faith, a faith that holds the redemptive and exemplary suffering of Jesus Christ at its core. I believe that faith to be both gift and habit, though the gift may sometimes feel like a cross to be borne and the habit may slip from the well-grooved action of virtue to the mindless repetition of routine.

In fact, it might be more accurate to say that my faith *began* as cross and repetition, the unpleasant childhood fact of What You Do on Sunday. How sad I was at age four when our family stopped attending Mass at the Newman Center at Cortland State, the upstate New York university where my father teaches, and began filling a pew at St. Mary's, a gray stone Gothic at the far end of Main Street. The Newman Center had an actual jungle gym in its basement where the very young could play while their parents worshipped. St. Mary's had a basement but no jungle gym, and I had to stay with my parents and my older brother Mark. Great was my relief in those days when we reached the Profession of Faith; it meant we were halfway through.

When did it become more than routine? What was the first intimation that religion was something other than a place our family went on Sunday mornings, something besides an altogether ordinary part of our lives? I remember my second year of CCD classes, the religious education program for Catholic kids who didn't attend St. Mary's parochial school. There, at seven, I won the big set of thin-tipped markers for being the first in my class to memorize and recite the Our Father, the Hail Mary, and the Apostle's Creed. It was no great achievement; I had been saying the first two for years, and was good at memorizing. But those thin tips were very adult, and winning carried its usual thrill. In that instance, however, religion was something you did to get something else, much as my own children stay quiet during Mass so that they will get a donut afterwards. I was no prodigy of piety. I feared eternity, even in heaven. "I think there should be a time when my spirit dies out," I once told my father as he tucked me into bed. "Mom says that when my spirit leaves my body, it will still feel like me, but I don't think it will."

I was, however, naturally curious about this all-powerful, eternal God. By age five, I was peppering Dad with questions.

"Dad, which is more powerful, nature or God?"

"Which do you think is more powerful?"

I went with my experience. "Nature, because nature makes storms, and storms are more powerful than God."

Three weeks later: "Dad, does God make tornadoes?'

"That's a hard question. God does make nature, and nature operates according to certain laws, and sometimes those laws produce a tornado."

"I still think nature is more powerful than God."

I wondered about the outcome of a battle between Jesus and the devil in hell. On earth, it seemed, the fight was going to Satan. My father once had to sit me down for several pre-Christmas scoldings, asking me, "If God were sitting right here, what would you tell him you're going to try to do to prepare your heart for Jesus' coming this Christmas?"

"It's no use Dad. I'm just always getting into trouble. I'm going to have to run away."

"You mean . . . in trouble with Mom and me?"

"Yes. I'm *always* getting into trouble. I'm going to run away, *really*. I'm just tired of all this trouble."

"Well, look," my father said. "What do you think we could do about all this trouble?"

"We can't do anything, because the devil is too strong. I think he's the strongest thing there is—we can't beat him."

Still, by the time I won those markers, faith had begun to take hold. Our family watched the ballyhooed PBS series *Cosmos*. The host, Carl Sagan, was a professed nonbeliever who equated religious belief with a prescientific worldview. Sagan concluded one long, awestruck tribute to the wonders of the universe with the phrase, ". . . the star stuff that we are made of." I narrowed my eyes at the screen and pronounced, "Wrong! We're made of *God*!"

But faith is not the formal practice of religion. I remember trying to think up sins to confess at my first reconciliation, though I don't recall the actual event. Nor do I recall my first communion. I do remember my grandmother giving me a rosary afterwards, just before we entered the local Holiday Inn for a celebratory brunch. These twenty-three years later—I am thirty-one now—I still have the rosary. The silver chain between the black wood beads has been repaired once or twice, and when the flimsy silver crucifix at the rosary's base broke off, I replaced it with a much more beautiful one, found in a California antique shop.

The new one is thick, substantial: silver inlaid with black wood. The crucified Christ, though rubbed smooth in a few places, is still detailed enough to reveal the woven crown of thorns; the folds of the loincloth; the gaunt, mournful face. Tiny nails pierce the hands and pin Christ to the wood of the cross. Another supports the base beneath His feet, and a fourth tacks up the scroll bearing His title. I am not embarrassed to talk of one crucifix being more beautiful than another; I *am* embarrassed to admit that I have never, with any regularity, taken the twenty minutes a day to say the prayers associated with the beads. The sense of faith didn't start there.

ᴓᴓᴓᴓᴓ

A BETTER POSSIBILITY would be sixth-grade CCD. In sixth grade, our teacher was Phil Evangelista. He was not like other men. In our staid, largely Irish parish, he was a spirited, thick-trunked Italian, somehow in our midst instead of across town at St. Anthony's. He wore shirts open at the collar, with wide lapels that splayed out over the front of his suit jacket. He wore a great gold crucifix on the outside of his suit. And he had religion; he burned for Jesus.

I don't know how Mr. Evangelista ended up teaching CCD. He was older, maybe retired, but still vital. He had a workshop in the church basement. In later days, I sometimes imagined he used the room to store the remnants of our gorgeous church's pre–Vatican II past: the marble communion rail, the throne-like wooden priests' chairs, the gold door of the reredos's walled-up tabernacle. He was the building's janitor, repairing the pews, mopping the floor, polishing the ponderous gold candlesticks that flanked the lower altar until they were replaced with simpler, humbler, more modern versions made of wood and black iron.

What he taught is mostly lost to me, except for his claim that God instituted only two sacraments, baptism and the Eucharist, while man created the other five. What I remember is the man: his gleaming white hair swept back against his head; his powerful features and barking, strangely accented voice; his hands. Mr. Evangelista had the biggest knuckles I had ever seen, but that wasn't the first thing you noticed about his hands, or at least the right hand. The first thing was that he was missing one finger entirely, and another above the middle. He told us he had lost all four fingers in a machine accident, and had then picked them up and marched to the hospital, where he sat, fingers in hand, waiting for them to be reattached. The surgery was not entirely successful; besides the segments that had to be removed, he had no feeling in any of what remained. To demonstrate, he would smash his fingers against the tabletop, backhanding those big knuckles into the wood with alarming force.

WHY DID HE DO THAT? Why did he tell us that story with such vehemence? I always thought he was trying to get our attention, but I don't think it was just a parlor trick. I think what he did had something to do with what he wanted to tell us, something terribly important connected to his maimed and senseless hand. His talk was full of disappointment and dismay at the state of the world. When he contrasted the old days—days when Sunday reception of communion required you to start fasting at midnight on Saturday—with the current policy of a mere one-hour fast, a policy that allowed people to receive "with the smell of alcohol still on their breath," his rage was palpable. He was laid open, vulnerable and raw with emotion. It was strange coming from so powerful a man. It made me uncomfortable.

I was twelve, on the verge of becoming a teenager and wary of emotional self-exposure. But he was impossible for me to dismiss, even if I didn't understand him. Looking back, I think he was telling us that something was wrong and that we needed to pay attention if we were to figure out what it was. Then maybe we would understand his talk about Jesus. He was a signalman. I couldn't read the signal, but I knew it meant something.

⟋⟍⟋⟍⟋⟍⟋⟍⟋⟍

are you still having sex?

AS ADOLESCENCE GATHERED ON THE HORIZON, I got my first intimations that being Catholic meant being Other in ways besides Mass on Sundays and fish on Fridays. I was not raised in an environment that spent time distinguishing between the faithful and those outside the fold, so I had never given much thought to the faith of my friends. As far as I knew, none of them were Catholic, but the knowledge was neither pleasant nor bothersome. We never discussed religion; we were too busy arguing over who shot who first when we played war.

Then came sex.

A bunch of us sixth graders played Truth or Dare after school under a low canopy of pine trees in Cortland's Beaudry Park. Everybody was nervous, so nobody demanded anything too extreme, lest they be subjected to the same request. The furthest that things went was some boy being commanded to moon the group, or a boy and a girl to French kiss. I stuck to Truth and was generally left alone, which was how I wanted it. I didn't go to the pine trees to drop my pants or practice kissing. I went because it was exciting just to be close to anything even vaguely sexual. But I knew that was as far as I'd go—close to it.

It's hard to say how much of that conviction was religious and how much was the Irish propriety I absorbed from my mother. By seventh grade, however, when the couples started pairing off and "going down," as we called it, there was a definite religious element to my holding back. I remember being consulted by a thirteen-year-old fellow Catholic about exactly how far he could go. He wanted me to make the careful distinctions that would allow him to stay right with God and still get action. Somehow, I hit upon the notion that everything was basically okay except intercourse (save sex for marriage!), a judgment he received happily enough.

But I held myself to a different standard. I had resolved never to "do more than kiss a girl." I did this not because I possessed some secret understanding of sin in general or lust in particular, not because I had an especial fear of hell, but because that was the limit my brother had told me he employed. In those days, if Mark said it, it was pretty much Gospel.

ᴐᴐᴐᴐᴐ

MARK IS FIVE AND A HALF YEARS OLDER than I am. My mother is fond of pointing out that in nearly every photo in which

I am a baby and Mark is present, I am looking at him. That fascination grew into a deep devotion, of which my brother was wonderfully tolerant. After I admired the wooden hand-gun he had made in wood shop—we were living in Boston at the time, and he and his friends played war in the hotel parking garage across the street—he made one for me. For my Christmas present that year, he fashioned and painted a wooden Spider-Man doll, complete with movable arms and dowel joints at the hips and knees.

Even when he turned moody at age thirteen, he put up with me. Graciously, he allowed me to share his enthusiasms: I listened to his old-time radio recordings of "The Shadow" and "Jack Benny," read his prized X-Men and Daredevil comic books, and even sat in while he and his eighth-grade buddies played Dungeons & Dragons. As I made my way through high school and he through college, we developed a shared sense of humor, a delight in rewriting pop songs and poking fun at the culture in general. (Mom thought us cynical and blamed our collections of *Mad Magazine* and Peanuts. "Of course the dog is the cynic," she said of Snoopy. Only later, when I discovered that "cynic" also meant "of or pertaining to the Dog Star," did I understand her understanding of Peanuts. Though by then, I had learned that even the funnies could be deeply tied up with a particular view of God and humanity.) When Mark married in 1991, I wept, fearing a weakening of the bond between us. He had to take a moment to console me before leaving his wedding reception: "It's not like I'm dead, Matt."

I needn't have feared. As the years passed, we became more like peers, and we grew closer still, though differences began to show. Mark, who went on to get his master's in theology, was more cerebral than I, more inclined to identify ideas with persons. After I started college, we began to argue about theology, a running debate that culminated in his dissatisfaction with my senior thesis, a defense of St. Thomas Aquinas's fourth proof for the existence of God. He feared that I had reduced Thomas to a Christian glosser of Aristotle, that I failed to appreciate the difference that being a Christian makes, even (perhaps especially) in matters of intellect. He feared that our unity—as brothers and friends—had been compromised by my intellectual formation.

I was amazed to learn this. I saw his point—ideas can certainly drive people apart, and ideas about theology, the preeminent science, mattered more than most. But theology didn't go to the heart of me the way it did with Mark. We were pulling our own version of *The School of Athens*—Mark as Plato, pointing heavenward to indicate the supreme importance of ideas, me as Aristotle, hand held low to emphasize our fraternal relation. In the end, we mended the rift (if not the disagreement) over a night's talk and a few shared rounds of bourbon at a restaurant bar.

BUT THAT WAS LATER. At twelve, Mark was still the standard. He left for Notre Dame just as I was entering junior high. I am certain I repeated many of his adolescent missteps, and I know I took a fair number that were all my own. But there were others I avoided, thanks to his various counsels, particularly in matters sexual. So if high school was not exactly a great spiritual awakening—I don't think I went to confession during those years—neither was it a corrupting wallow in the irreligious muck. I was no champion of purity, but I muddled through without breaking my resolution: I fell in love, but I never did more than kiss a girl. And if you've never tasted the forbidden fruit of sex, it's easier to contemplate never tasting it at all. By senior year, I was thinking of becoming a priest.

There was some adolescent absolutism about my desire. I was eager to spend my life in the service of Christ. (I didn't care so much for the name "Jesus" back then—too soft.) How best to serve? The only thing to do is the best thing, the priesthood is the best thing, QED. There was also some hero-worship and romanticism. G. K. Chesterton's little book on St. Francis, read before I made my mid-senior-year journey to Rome and Assisi, charmed me utterly with its depiction of a love of creation born from a wholehearted, even impassioned love of the Creator. There was a desire to give better sermons than I was used to hearing. And I hope there was some genuine piety in the mix. But I think that mainly, there was a desire to step out of the mainstream.

Like a lot of adolescents, I placed a great value on non-conformity. I had always enjoyed being the odd man out in a group—the catcher in baseball, the goalie in hockey, the only tuba in the band. In high school, that list grew to include the Catholic who stayed a virgin, who didn't decide that the faith was all a crock or that it simply wasn't worth thinking about. I had my difficulties: shortly before receiving the sacrament of Confirmation, a sacrament I neither particularly desired nor understood, I told my father that I wasn't sure I believed in God. He took my doubts seriously, and sought out a series of videos entitled *Jesus: Then and Now*, which we watched and discussed. By the end, my faith was bolstered; I concentrated on the Incarnation, and found I could believe. But I never took my adolescent doubt as a sign that I should necessarily reject my Catholicism. I was almost certainly too young to experience a dark night of the soul, but I knew that great saints had suffered them. They had felt cut off from God, unable to find Him anywhere, and had persevered.

Whatever the quality of my faith, I continued to practice my religion and adhere to its teachings, and that was enough to brand me in the public eye. When some friends nicknamed me Captain Catholic, it was irritating, but was there not also some secret pleasure in being singled out? *I'm the rebel; I'm the nonconformist.* When I wrote an angry teenage poem about truth and sheep and death and lies, a friend assumed I was expressing disgust with thoughtless followers of the Good Shepherd. Nothing so subtle or close to home: I was going after my classmates. The mainstream, as I saw it, was choked with a sludge of alcohol and sex. (I didn't avoid the former as well as I did the latter, but neither did I make a habit of it.)

Besides my brother's influence, I had my father's learned reasoning to back me up on this. He was a developmental psychologist who specialized in the moral formation of children—our two-year stay in Boston gave him time to work with Lawrence Kohlberg, a giant in the field. Carefully and calmly, through argument and example, he had convinced me that premarital sex was the wrongful use of another person for self-gratification.

My own experience corroborated his teaching. Perhaps because I lacked a predatory air, I ended up being friends with a number of girls, and I got to see up close the effects of at least one postcoital breakup. I saw that sex could do damage. Athletic locker rooms gave me a chance to compare that girl's misery to the cheerful rut-talk of guys amongst themselves. (Not that the rut-talk didn't grip my ears. There's a reason we're asked to reject the *glamour* of sin when we renew our baptismal vows.) I swallowed a lot of dirty water, and by the end of high school, I was ready to inhabit some purer medium.

So when I started telling people during my senior year that I was planning on becoming a priest, it was partly out of mischief—not a doctor, lawyer, or engineer, folks, but a *priest*, something this town hasn't produced in a generation—partly for the reasons I have mentioned, and partly out of a simple distaste for sex. The *idea* of sex still had tremendous appeal: I liked girls fine—I had even loved one—and I had my share of imaginary trysts with fantastic sirens. But I balked at even the thought of actual sex with an actual person. Too damaging—to both of us.

Mark used to tease me that when married couples came to me for priestly counsel, I would ask, "Are you still having sex?"

"Yes, Father."

"Well, then, there's your problem."

‿‿‿‿‿

AN UNHEALTHY ATTITUDE (and an un-Catholic one), born of too much time spent in an unhealthy clime. College was my saving grace here. I attended Thomas Aquinas College, a lay-founded Catholic liberal arts school with a curriculum built around the Great Books. The women I met and fell in love with there were not mousy prudes. To me, they were vivacious and fascinating, by turns sophisticated, bawdy, and sweet—women who drank and smoked and exuded life. They were also Catholics who regarded chastity as a virtue. Sex, the pleasure and intimacy of it, wasn't the problem; sex torn out of the context of marriage and family was the problem. Even the pious girls in chapel veils who went on rosary walks with boys around the campus ponds (an admittedly extraordinary sight in 1991) didn't strike me as repressed. They loved something—someone—and so sought to please Him with their behavior. Many girls carried a book into the chapel entitled *This Tremendous Lover*. It took me a while to figure out that the lover was Christ and not some paperback romance Casanova.

Before I fell in love—and it only took a few weeks after my arrival—I expressed my priestly intentions to the college chaplain, Father Steckler. Father was a lean, ropy, white-haired Jesuit who tromped about campus in a black cassock but wore shorts for his goatlike ascents into the surrounding mountains. He liked Bombay Sapphire gin and cigars, and he was fond of cooking fine meals for small groups of students in the priests' residence.

I liked him immediately: the orderly workings of his mind, the staccato rasp of his voice, the cheerful scorn—sharpened by age and experience—that he heaped upon the enemies of the church. When I said I wanted to be a priest, Father told me to wait until the end of junior year, and if I was still interested, to come and see him about it again.

A visiting priest from the Legionaries of Christ got to me some time before that. I knew him a little, and my mother and I had attended his ordination in Rome. He gave me a talk about "giving God the first shot"—entering the seminary to "test my vocation" before contemplating marriage. That's what he had done, and he had left a girl behind to do it. It broke his heart, he told me, but he decided he had to give God the first shot. Now, here he was, a priest of God and no regrets.

I didn't know how to answer him, but I balked at following his counsel. I was a great one for fulfilling the duties imposed by religion, but my vocation seemed outside the realm of obligation. I had first considered the priesthood based on the leanings of my heart. Now, my heart was leading me elsewhere. I was in love with a woman, and the idea of rejecting that love to make way for another seemed strange. If I had a vocation to the priesthood, I thought, shouldn't I *want* to be a priest? Shouldn't there be a nagging, inescapable force at work on my will, a sense that I was not where I ought to be? I prayed about his advice, but not too hard. I was afraid at the force of his argument, but I no longer felt the priesthood's tug on my soul. What I felt was earthly love for a good woman. By the end of junior year—the time Father Steckler had set for me to talk to him about the priesthood—I had met the woman who would become my wife.

Now I have sons of my own, three of them. I would love to see one or more of them on the altar one day, ordained priests saying the Mass. Getting them there will not be easy. I still believe that personal desire plays a part in discerning one's vocation. But it does seem to me that God's call to the priesthood is coming as a still, small voice these days, one easily drowned out by the whirlwinds and earthquakes of the world. My boys will need help to hear it. Once, the vocations director for the San Diego diocese gave a sermon at our parish. His talk was squishy, walk-with-Jesus stuff—squishy because everyone is called to walk with Jesus. You don't have to be a priest to do that.

I could have stood something stronger, especially given the atmosphere surrounding the priesthood in the wake of the abuse scandal. Who would want to become a priest today, unless he understood that sacrifice was essential to the calling, and that the world's hatred (or at least its scorn) was par for the course? Celibacy is regarded by some as stifling at best, deeply damaging at worst. I could have stood some of the old Church Militant talk—we need soldiers for Christ, men who will lay down their lives so that others may live in the grace of our Lord (though Lord knows, I never heard it put this way when I was growing up). The job of the church is to lead souls to heaven. The sacraments are the food for that journey, and we need priests for the sacraments. Confession, the Mass, the Eucharist—these are the things unique to priests. These are the reasons we need them.

I don't think we're going to see an end to the rule of celibacy. I do think this is a moment of crisis for the priesthood in this country. So many gray heads on the altar. Around my hometown of Cortland, there is talk of a cluster of parishes: many parishes served by one priest, saying Mass here one Sunday, there the next.

Priests come from families. The families of those who oppose celibacy—and hesitate over obedience in general—will likely not produce many priests to replace the current ranks. Those families that support and revere the priesthood as it is defined by the church, those parents who can encourage their sons to listen for a call that requires the sacrifice of marital love, will likely produce more. Hope springs eternal.

⋙

too much kissing with father dave

IN 1993, I GOT MY FIRST WHIFF of the priestly sexual abuse scandal; I started hearing people talk about Jason Berry's *Lead Us Not into Temptation: Catholic Priests and the Sexual Abuse of Children.* The problem, astonishing as it seemed to pious ears, was apparently widespread. But my particular experience of the scandal came years earlier. When I was about fourteen years old, I was kissed by a priest: Father Dave.

The act did not have the character of an assault, but of a line crossed; he was affectionate with lots of youngsters—from kids to teenagers—in ways that few people thought inappropriate. He was every kid's favorite, the young-at-heart associate pastor who paid attention to us.

"You have a musical head. Did you know that?" he liked to ask the small ones.

"What do you mean, Father?"

"Listen." He squeezed your forehead and puffed out his lips with air so that a tiny squeak escaped, to your delight. "See? A musical head." Then he tucked his hands under your arms and tossed you into the air. After you landed, he hugged you close and said, "You're a BP—a beautiful person. Who loves you?"

"You do, Father."

"Do you know who else loves you? Jesus loves you." Then he kissed your forehead. All this was after Mass, Father still in his vestments, filling up those frustrating minutes after church when parents milled about on the sidewalk, chatting and laughing and not going to the car.

None of this affection felt creepy at the time. It felt wonderful, and it made Father Dave very attractive. He preached one of the only sermons I can remember from my childhood. It had the character of an old chestnut. Father described a world where people carried their hearts in their hands. One man sought to keep his heart perfect and unsullied, and kept it protected in a glass box. Another man was forever exchanging pieces of his heart with others. His heart became lumpy and ugly to look upon—none of the pieces fit just so. But he was happy. Old chestnut or no, love made me listen and remember.

When we got to be teenagers, Father took us on "Blood Baths"—visits to the college racquetball courts, where he excelled despite his paunch. If there were four of us, we played basketball afterwards; often, we went swimming in the college's indoor pool. The only oddity—and it only occasionally felt like an oddity—was the way he gently insisted on everybody showering afterwards in the locker room. Then we all went to Friendly's restaurant for ice cream sundaes. Going on a Blood Bath was cool, a kind of honor. Even non-Catholics joined in. I loved Blood Baths, and was happy when Father Dave continued to come back for them even after he was transferred to another parish.

IT WAS DURING ONE OF THESE LATER OUTINGS, one that involved just the two of us, that he kissed me. It was not strange for him to hug me between points, to tell me he loved me and that I was a beautiful person. He had been doing that for years. But this time, his hug grew tighter, so that I could feel the hard strength in his arms. His kisses moved from my forehead to my lips, where tiny pecks gave way to one long pressing of his mouth to mine. If my memory serves, I froze, went rigid, and said nothing. The moment passed, and we resumed our game. The freezing feeling remained. My father recalls that after I got home and he asked me how the game went, I replied rather coolly, "Too much hugging and kissing."

"Kissing? What kind of kissing—you mean, on the lips?"

"Yes."

"How many times?"

"Fifteen to twenty."

My father immediately went into his study and began writing a letter to Father Dave. It took him several days to finish. In the letter, he said he didn't want to believe that the event betrayed a more serious problem. But when it came time to send it, my father realized that he had a responsibility to bring the matter before the bishop. So he made an appointment and presented the letter. My father could see the pain in the bishop's face as he read. The bishop said he was very sorry for what had happened. He said that he had had complaints from other parishioners about Father Dave's "excessive" displays of affection toward children. He said that he would meet with Father Dave and show him the letter, which he did. Shortly thereafter, Father was moved into chaplain work with the elderly.

A few years after that, and soon after the installation of a new bishop, the diocese was sued because Father Dave had molested two other boys, ages ten and eleven. (This had happened before his encounter with me, while he was at the other parish. The case was settled out of court. As part of the settlement, the diocese agreed to provide a letter from the new bishop, reading, "Please accept this letter as an apology for any unfortunate happenings which you feel may have happened to you and your family stemming from your participating in church activities.")

෴෴෴෴

MY FAITH WAS NOT SHAKEN BY MY ENCOUNTER—or at least, if it was, I wasn't aware of it. Father Dave was not the church. Father Dave was a poor sinner, like the rest of us. The truth the church proclaims, and my docility to that church, would not be altered even if it came out that the pope himself was a molester—though in that case, I think my heart would break. I didn't dwell on Father's advances, and I continued to think about becoming a priest myself.

In recent times, as news of priestly wrongdoing has burst into the headlines (and continued to ooze out in a fetid trickle), I have not been driven into a helpless, strangled rage. I didn't really suffer from my encounter with an abusive priest, not the way others have suffered. Once, soon after my encounter with Father Dave, I broke down in sobs at the dining-room table, but the tears came and went and didn't come back. It was easy for me to forgive Father Dave; easy to feel nothing but pity and sorrow when I heard that he had left the priesthood and later died of AIDS; easy to think of his sin as a terrible weakness, rather than an evil habit that caused incredible damage to young lives.

What upsets me is the hierarchy's reaction. I can understand wayward flesh, even wayward flesh that violates the young. But when the response from the pastors of that wayward flesh is defensive, and gives the impression of one episcopal eye being cast toward the courtroom—can't admit too much, lest it be used in a lawsuit—I have a harder time forgiving. It seems a more spiritual failing on the part of our spiritual leaders. It looks to me like men abandoning their posts as shepherds of souls and turning into politicians. I read where a spokesman for the U.S. Bishops' Conference said, "This is not Watergate; it's Whitewater." He was claiming that the problem was not as bad as it was being depicted, but the political analogy struck me as both telling and in bad taste. Though the scandals have a political character, they stem from intimate, personal events. The damage is also personal, devastatingly so.

When I heard the early claims from the hierarchy that the media was distorting the issue, or that things are better now than they were, or that the trouble stemmed from too much trust in therapy, I thought of Clinton's televised semi-apology during the Lewinsky scandal. Instead of a simple, "I'm sorry I lied," we got a reminder that his lie had come during a deposition for a case that never went to court. Both Clinton and the bishops may have been telling the truth. But people were not satisfied with Clinton's dodge, and he eventually broke down and gushed his mea culpas. Similarly, many victims I read about hungered for genuine contrition, not explanation, from their bishops. (Eventually, in some cases, it came.)

I wanted to protest. I wanted to stop giving money to my diocese. I was ready to see the diocese of Boston go bankrupt as a result of the lawsuits brought against it. However sobering it was to think that such an event might mean the closing of schools, hospitals, and charitable services, I was ready to sacrifice them all if bankruptcy would shock the bishops into serious action. Sin has consequences, I said to myself. It's folly to pretend otherwise.

OUTRAGE MAKES IT EASIER to hold such extreme opinions. Outrage is wearying, however, and difficult to maintain. Now, I would rather see the church limp along, doing what good it can, than watch it collapse under the weight of its own failings. But if it is difficult to maintain outrage, it can also be difficult to maintain faith in those responsible.

I have heard that the present age has been called "the hour of the laity." I think the idea is that the laity have been called upon to act as full members of the Body of Christ, to do His work and spread His gospel and not simply look to priests and religious to transform the world. If outrage gives way to despair in our leaders' ability to lead us on the path to Christ, it could become a different sort of "hour of the laity." One in which priests are valued only insofar as they dispense the sacraments, and bishops are valued not at all. Such an hour would, I think, be a dark one for the church.

I take comfort in the thought that the church has had dark hours before. So many brief accounts of the saints seem to mention that the blessed soul, while still on earth, "worked for the reform of the church." Thanks to the persistence of sin, the edifice has been crumbling since it was first built, and again and again, God has brought good out of evil. My brother, echoing my own hopes, puts it bluntly: "To be a priest now is to live under a cloud of scandal. Men who enter the priesthood today will need to be men of true faith, who know that following Christ means sharing in His crucifixion."

৶ ৶ ৶ ৶ ৶

the poisonous tentacles of anti-abortion zealots

HELPING THE POOR was my first introduction to the political dimension of the faith, the part that follows Jesus' second great commandment to love your neighbor as yourself, the part that seeks to transform the world through the love of Christ. I learned from my father. He has always been for me a model of quiet generosity, forever giving away both money and time to those who ask. Growing up, our obligation to the less fortunate was axiomatic, like Mass on Sunday. The idea took hold. At dinner, he read the letters from our foster children overseas, as well as the solicitations from charities such as Oxfam America, Amnesty International, and Covenant House. When I was six, our family heard a priest at the Boston University chapel (Dad was a visiting professor there for two years) encourage families to consider fasting for one meal a week and donating the money saved to the poor. On the way home from Mass, I proposed we do just that. We kept up the tradition for years.

Helping the poor was the first introduction. Abortion was the second.

As my father saw it, the argument was chiefly about whether the unborn were among our neighbors, and if so, what was to be done about it. Dad held that the fetus was a person, and that a person's right to life had to come first. Without the right to life, all other rights—including that of the pregnant woman's privacy—were meaningless. For a time, the question of whether the government had a right to intervene in the matter seemed less clear. But by the time I was twelve, Dad had come to understand the church's full teaching that, besides being a serious personal sin, abortion was a grave social injustice that we as citizens were obliged to oppose. I know because I heard him arguing with a friend of mine who had come to visit; it was the first I had ever heard of abortion. I couldn't understand why this kid, my old pal from our family's two years in Boston, was arguing with my father.

I ONCE WROTE AN ESSAY ABOUT MY FATHER that began with a quote from Ecclesiastes: "There is nothing better for a man but that he should eat and drink and find enjoyment in his toil. This also, I saw, is from the hand of God." My dad toils a lot, almost more than I can believe. I can recall eighteen-hour days, Mom calling downstairs at two or three in the morning for him to quit his desk and come upstairs. It is not uncommon to step into his study and find him stretched out on the floor, perfectly composed and looking not unlike a corpse in state, snatching a few minutes of sleep before returning to his computer. He is not a workaholic; work does not fill in for the goods of God and family. (He spends time each morning in prayer, and often attends daily Mass. Growing up, any car ride longer than fifteen minutes provided the occasion for a quick family rosary. And familial intimacy has been a constant goal, the driving force behind the vast sums spent to bring the family together for vacations, the nightly topics at the dinner table, the constant encouragement of questions about each other's lives.) But Lord, how he works.

He works like that because his work has the character of a cause. As a specialist in the moral development of children, Dad has become a leader in the effort to restore character education to the mission of the public schools. (Poor me, whose father wrote a book entitled *Raising Good Children*. Poor Dad, whose son was sent home from school for biting a girl on the ankle the day he appeared on *The Merv Griffin Show* to promote that book.) He spends part of every month on the road, giving workshops here, conducting research there. He is deeply hopeful in the face of bleak reality, and he is fiercely committed.

He brought that same commitment to the abortion issue. I spent more than one late-eighties afternoon seated at the side table in the living room, stuffing envelopes with Dad's latest comment—half to newspapers around New York State, half to major newspapers around the country. Dad fought on his home turf as well. He wrote letters to the *Cortland Standard*, prayed rosaries in front of the local clinic where abortions were performed. When it came out that the high school's counselors were referring girls to the clinic and sending them there, on school time, without notifying parents, my father helped back a candidate for the school board who opposed the practice.

It was the revoking of the Father Drumm Award that got the pro-choice crowd really upset. The local branch of Catholic Charities gave out the medal at its annual awards dinner. In 1991, they announced their intention to present it to a woman who was a prominent signer of two full-page ads in the *Cortland Standard* supporting abortion rights. My father and some other pro-life Catholics felt moved to protest. Though the woman had been involved in many humanitarian activities, Dad thought the church should not bestow honors on those who contradicted its teaching. He was one of nineteen signers of a letter to the board of Catholic Charities and to the bishop. Catholic Charities never responded, but the bishop intervened the night before the ceremony to revoke the award. The *Standard* gave the story front-page treatment, and the day's editorial blasted "anti-abortion zealots who were determined to wrap their poisonous tentacles around something so wholesome as community service."

Over the next ten days, the paper also ran numerous letters, most of which attacked my father's motives and called him names. He was accused of being a hateful right-winger. Dad was a registered Democrat, a man who had marched in Washington because he believed the war in Vietnam was unjust. As he saw it, the Democratic party had abandoned its role as champion of the oppressed when it decided not to defend the rights of the helpless unborn. He was no right-winger, and there was no hatred in his heart. But he made no reply.

"Blessed are you when men revile you and persecute you and utter all kinds of evil against you falsely on my account. Rejoice and be glad, for your reward is great in heaven, for so men persecuted the prophets who were before you" (Matthew 5:11–12). I have always thought that a skeptic would be tempted to regard that line as gasoline on the flames of a martyr complex, divine balm for a bruised ego. But in my father's silence, I saw not ego, but holiness.

Though I agreed with my father about abortion, I did not share his zeal, his willingness to soldier on. Once, as a teenager, I hurt him deeply by complaining that abortion was all we ever talked about. I joked with my brother, Mark, about waking the old man some morning:

"Hey Dad, time to get up."

"Mmnh? 'Bortion."

MY OWN EFFORTS at defending the pro-life position did not go well. I lacked my father's range of knowledge, his rhetorical skill, and his humility. Debates with my friend Steven quickly had me repeating myself, wondering why he couldn't see the truth of my argument.

Another encounter gave rise to a particularly embarrassing testament to my fallen nature. Mrs. Simms was one of my favorite teachers and a remarkable woman. Tall, thin, and large-eyed, she had short, styled hair that swooped and dipped about the top of her head and a fabulous wardrobe highlighted by a number of sweeping shawls and capes. She looked to me like a great, noble bird—a heron, or an egret. I thought her warm and gracious with us unruly adolescents, but she was capable of inspiring awe when she so desired.

She was my teacher for Advanced Placement American History, and she gave our little group considerable room to play as long as we got our work done. She was also my teacher for You and the Law, a more hurly-burly general-requirement civics course where she flexed her grand authority. When the class arrived at the subject of abortion, Mrs. Simms expressed sympathy for the pro-life position, but ultimately sided with the rights of the pregnant woman. I spoke up in opposition. I feared my classmates would accept without question the word of so glamorous and imposing a figure.

Apparently, many of them already shared her views. What followed was a round of me against the world, giving standard answers to standard objections and getting impassioned in the face of general opposition. The next day, the tranquility of our history class was broken by the ring of the classroom telephone. After she hung up, Mrs. Simms called me out into the hall, visibly upset. The call had come from the mother of a girl in my You and the Law class. The girl had come home crying, so intimidated was she by my argumentation. As far as I knew, I hadn't even spoken directly to her. Mrs. Simms was angry with me for reducing this girl to tears. I was angry with Mrs. Simms. She had started the whole thing by giving her opinion on the matter. I had been the only one on my side. *I* was intimidating? *I* was the bad guy?

My anger cooled; I had the peace of one who is certain he has done right, even if I didn't do it with much grace or effectiveness. What happened after that was not a crime of passion, nor was it the ugly fruit of cool, malicious premeditation. It was just a nasty impulse, a minor eruption of original sin. I was sitting against the outside of the school, waiting for a ride home. About thirty feet away, Mrs. Simms left the building and began walking toward her car. I lofted a pebble in her direction.

Nobody else was about; it was very quiet. She heard the stone hit the sidewalk and skitter away. She turned to face me.

"Did you just throw a rock at me?"

I had been in a sort of fugue, acting without thought. The question brought me back to myself, and I looked back on what had just happened with horrified wonder. What had I done?

I wanted to defend myself. *It wasn't a rock; it was a pebble. I didn't throw it at you; I threw it near you, in your general direction.*

And I didn't throw *it; I just sort of—tossed it.* But however much I qualified it, the miserable reality remained. There was nothing to do but apologize. To her great credit, Mrs. Simms forgave me, and even wrote me a letter of recommendation for college, one that left out my attempted stoning.

ぷぷぷぷぷ

my dad and *the plague*

I GREW UP IN CORTLAND, but I liked to hang out in nearby Ithaca, on the Commons. The Commons is a stretch of State Street open only to pedestrians, its center filled with pavilions and play structures, its edges lined with shops and eateries. Cortland was a college town, but nearby Ithaca, home to both Cornell University and Ithaca College, was a much better college town. Ithaca had art-house theaters and arty types to fill them. Ithaca had beautiful Ivy League girls; I used to eat lunch by the window in Simeon's Restaurant at the Commons' edge and watch them go by in their long, elegant winter coats. And Ithaca had young punks—spiked mohawks in neon pink and green, black leather boots and jackets, studs and chains and safety pins—who hung out on one of the pavilions. I was a would-be arty type myself, and I loved just being there.

Of all the art theaters in Ithaca, Cinemapolis was perhaps the funkiest—certainly the most subterranean. Deep under the Commons it lay, a hive of tiny theaters, some with what seemed like only twenty seats. It was in the smallest of these that I saw my father split in two on-screen, the two disparate halves that find union in his persona separated and given life.

The movie was Yves Robert's *My Father's Glory*, based on Marcel Pagnol's novels about his childhood in France. Eleven-year-old Marcel is the narrator, and it is immediately clear that he worships his father, Joseph. Joseph is a schoolteacher, a lover of reason and a firm believer in the idea that science will eventually explain everything. Religion to him is superstition, the enemy of reason and truth. He is outraged by the idea of the Eucharist, of God in a wafer and a cup, consumed all over the world at Mass.

Joseph is trim, disciplined, and intense; very much in love with his wife and son, but also devoted to his work and the life of the mind. At the film's outset, there does not seem to be a naturally self-indulgent bone in his body. He is a secular ascetic.

Joseph is my father: a believer in science and rigor. A great observer of details, hesitant to make any statement he cannot cite evidence to support. Always, I am asked, "Where did you read that?" "What were his exact words?" Superstition and confusion are anathema; my father's work as a psychologist and educator is good, in part, because he is so careful not to spin theories out of air, but to draw conclusions only from what he sees. He is a great believer in the light of reason, and docile to truth wherever he recognizes it. And the physical resemblance between Joseph and Dad is significant—the spare frame hinting at some immaterial fire that consumes the flesh and its smothering desires.

In the film, Joseph finds his opposite in Uncle Jules, his wife's brother-in-law and a genial French Catholic. Uncle Jules is fat and happy, devout and untroubled. He has money, and is generous with it. While he willingly enters into verbal jousts with Joseph, it is clear that he sees little risk in the fight. He will not be unhorsed, no matter how telling the blow to his beliefs; he will not even take offense. Over the course of the film, Jules tempers Joseph's lofty intellectualism—he gets Joseph to enjoy wine and introduces him to the simple joys of hunting. Joseph, who spurns a village priest and the notion of being photographed with a trophy animal, eventually yields to both at once. By film's end, Joseph seems a little more human, and faith and reason seem a little less mutually exclusive.

Uncle Jules is also my father: secure in the peace that comes from faith in a loving God, sensitive to the earthly blessings of home and hearth. Grateful for the Lord's generosity in his own life, he finds it easy to be generous with others. Though he is forever testing ideas against his own understanding, there remains in him that one great idea that has mystery at its heart, the idea of faith. How do you test a mystery?

ONE WAY IS TO TEST IT AGAINST ITSELF, one part against another, and see if it holds together. "Lickona," according to my genealogist Uncle Chad, may be an Americanized form of the Alsatian name "Ligone." Watching *My Father's Glory*, I felt I was recognizing two aspects of native French temperament, aspects melded together in the character of my father, the careful thinker who still embraced his Christianity. Small wonder, then, that when I told my father I was reading Camus' *The Plague* in Senior English, he replied that it had long been his favorite novel. He compared Camus' prose to a scalpel, so precise were its movements, so clean the expression of its meaning. But the analogy needn't have stopped there. *The Plague*'s account of Father Paneloux's sermon on the suffering of children was cold, sharp metal on my warmest, tenderest parts.

ʃʷ ʃʷ ʃʷ ʃʷ ʃʷ

AFTER CENTURIES OF DORMANCY, the bubonic plague has broken out in the French city of Oran. The city is completely quarantined, closed off from the rest of the world. Death is everywhere. A priest, Father Paneloux, has already given one sermon that was equal parts warning and consolation. "The plague is the flail of God," he said then, "and the world His threshing floor, and implacably he will thresh out His harvest until the wheat is separated from the chaff." But he concluded by hoping against hope that "despite all the horrors of these dark days, despite the groans of men and women in agony, our fellow citizens would offer up to heaven that one prayer which is truly Christian, a prayer of love. And God would see to the rest."

Now, several months and many deaths later, Father is preaching again, this time at a Mass for men. He has invited his fellow citizen, the good Doctor Rieux, who tells Father that "until my dying day I shall refuse to love a scheme of things in which children are put to torture." Still, Rieux comes to the Mass, and sits in the church, and listens as a storm rages outside.

As Father Paneloux gets rolling with his sermon, he says that

the total acceptance of which he had been speaking was not to be taken in the limited sense usually given to the words; he was not thinking of mere resignation or even of that harder virtue, humility. It involved humiliation, but a humiliation to which the person humiliated gave full assent.

True, the agony of a child was humiliating to the heart and to the mind. But that was why we had to come to terms with it. And that, too, was why—and here Paneloux assured those present that it was not easy to say what he was about to say—since it was God's will, we, too, should will it.

Thus and thus only the Christian could face the problem squarely, and, scorning subterfuge, pierce to the heart of the supreme issue, the essential choice. And his choice would be to believe everything, so as not to be forced into denying everything. Like those worthy women who, after learning that buboes were the natural issues through which the body cast out infection, went to their church and prayed, 'Please, God, give him buboes,' thus the Christian should yield himself wholly to the divine will, even though it passed his understanding. It was wrong to say, 'This I understand, but that I cannot accept'; we must go straight to the heart of that which is unacceptable, precisely because it is thus that we are constrained to make our choice. The sufferings of children were our bread of affliction, but without this bread our souls would die of spiritual hunger.

Near the end of the sermon, Paneloux says,

My brothers . . . the love of God is a hard love. It demands total self-surrender, disdain of our human personality.

And yet it alone can reconcile us to suffering and the deaths of children, it alone can justify them, since we cannot understand them, and we can only make God's will ours. That is the hard lesson I would share with you today. That is the faith, cruel in men's eyes, and crucial in God's, which we must ever strive to compass. We must aspire beyond ourselves to that high and fearful vision. And on that lofty plane all will fall into place, all discords be resolved, and truth flash forth from the dark cloud of seeming injustice. (Albert Camus, *The Plague* [New York: The Modern Library, 1948])

I WAS OVERWHELMED. Camus, who clearly sympathized with the unbelieving doctor, struggling after meaning and morality in a world without God, had written the most powerful exposition of Christianity I had ever encountered. Father Paneloux was no raving zealot; earlier in the book, Camus called him "a stalwart champion of Christian doctrine at its most precise and purest, equally remote from modern laxity and the obscurantism of the past." In his sermon, the priest sought to manifest the awful price of maintaining Christianity's integrity. Like Paneloux, in effect if not in intention, Camus was forcing the hearer to look more closely at the terrible reality of the cross.

The intensity of adolescence heightened the sermon's stunning effect, and I found I couldn't write anything about the book for class. I certainly couldn't begin to critique Paneloux's theology, however harsh it seemed. I found I had none of the reader's distance; I was in that church, hearing that sermon, trying to bear its weight. My teacher, an ex-Trappist, kindly let my failure pass without consequence.

ᔧᔧᔧᔧᔧ

begging the sun to dance

WHILE STILL YOUNG ENOUGH to be deathly afraid of crocodiles under the bed, I received the following promise from my mother: "If there was a crocodile under your bed, I would come in and kill it with my bare hands." How deliciously shocking—my mother, the soul of retiring Irish gentleness, ripping out the monster's throat with bloodstained fingernails. The image was entirely incongruous, but I believed her promise absolutely.

Senior year, I learned something about the power of that kind of mother-love. Before I started talking seriously about the priesthood, I had talked about studying marine biology at the University of Miami. I had talked about applying to NYU to study acting. Then my mother said, "We'd really like it if you went to a Catholic college, one with single-sex dorms." Boom, that was that. I didn't even squawk. Up to that point, Catholic affiliation hadn't been a determining factor. Neither had the attempt to preserve chastity by making sure men and women slept apart. Now they became essential. I visited several schools, and ended up applying to only one—Thomas Aquinas College in Santa Paula, California.

When I had children of my own, I asked my mother how she had achieved such authority over me. "Sacrifice," was her immediate reply. "You knew we would do anything for you."

My mother is not given to statements so ringing with certitude, so when she does make them, they stick in my memory. Usually, they concern the faith. My mother's Catholicism is so deep-rooted as to sound matter-of-fact. She will say, without blinking, "You can't be happy without God." That used to drive me crazy. It used to drive her crazy as well, back when her own mother said it. It sounded parochial. It didn't acknowledge the complexities of human experience, the manifold particulars that clouded the soul's perception of its ultimate good.

Like Mom in her younger days, I protested. "Maybe people who know God are the happiest," I said, giving ground where I could. "Certainly, the saints seemed to share a great, secret joy. But there are plenty of people enjoying a normal, natural, human happiness without God." But Mom, like her mother before her, was not moved. She had come to believe her mother was right. People were made for God. If they didn't have him, they were, at the realest center of themselves, unhappy. Of course, she never said that, exactly. What she said was, "They may look happy, but really, they're not." It was her version of St. Augustine's, "Our hearts are restless until they rest in thee."

I DON'T KNOW EXACTLY when my mother accepted her own mother's teaching. I do know that for the first ten years of their marriage, both my parents (by their own embarrassed recollection) were content to live as Sunday Catholics. They did not pray daily, nor did they seek God's will for their lives. I don't know if they really sought God at all. When my father's college roommate—now a deacon—paid a visit to my parents, he was driven to say, "No offense, Tom, but I think you ought to read the Bible." My father replied by quoting the Episcopal bishop James Pike's version of the first commandment: "I am the Lord thy God; thou shall have no other gods before me—*including your concept of me.*" My father wasn't about to be roped into trying to know God, lest he start worshipping a false concept—a clever dodge.

Mom led the way out of these years of spiritual doldrums through her reading of C. S. Lewis. She read *Surprised by Joy*, Lewis's autobiography of faith. She read *Mere Christianity*. She read his sci-fi allegory *The Space Trilogy*, and she was especially moved by the third book, *That Hideous Strength,* because of its compelling depiction of spiritual warfare. Some of my earliest memories of being read to hail from about that time, when my mother introduced me to *The Chronicles of Narnia.* (After that, my father took over, taking me through Laura Ingalls Wilder's *Little House* books, *Tom Sawyer* and *Huckleberry Finn,* and *Watership Down.* But if my father read to me, it was my mother who led me to read. Countless pilgrimages to the library led to carefully placed caches of books about the house. "Just read the first chapter," she would say.) Dad followed Mom's lead by reading some Lewis, and also Sheldon Vanauken's *A Severe Mercy,* a conversion story in which Lewis played a major part. Then he pushed further, attending a men's retreat at a monastery in Philadelphia, which inspired him to take his first pokes at daily prayer. Now it was my mother's turn to follow, slipping prayer in at the start of her morning ritual of coffee and journal-writing in bed. She did not simply inherit her mother's piety and conviction; she developed them for herself.

However genuine it was, I still chafed at Mom's piety. I still do sometimes. The house I live in now is not the sort of house that people of my tax bracket can afford. We heard about it almost by accident from a friend, a real estate agent, about a half hour after it went on the market. We offered twenty thousand dollars less than another bidder. The owner accepted our offer because I wrote a letter explaining that we were young Catholics who wanted a large house and yard for a large family, and that we wanted room for grandparents to visit. Our own house sold twelve hours after we put it on the market, for more than our optimistic asking price. As I reported all these things to Mom over the phone, I could feel her waiting for me to acknowledge the workings of providence. I had already marveled to my wife that the divine fingerprints were all over this, but with Mom, my spirit turned impish. "It's almost as if there's a God," was the best I could do.

Mom sees God at work in many more places than I do—or if she doesn't see Him, she readily assumes His presence.

"God is taking care of you. He knows what's best for you."

"That's what they say, Ma," I jibed.

INTELLECTUALLY, IT'S NOT SUCH A REACH. "In Him we live and move and have our being," says St. Paul (Acts 17:28). He's everywhere, all the time. But she experiences Him, has a sense of His movement. What is my experience of God? It's not easy to say. I attend Mass on Sunday and Holy Days, pay some attention to the life of the church, try to teach the faith to my children and to deepen my own understanding. I struggle to improve my moral and spiritual life, to become, in the most unsappy way, a more loving person—a better imitation of

Christ. I am following Paul's counsel, working out my salvation in fear and trembling.

I have not sought the experience of God. I have never regarded it as an essential part of my faith. I tend to think that an experience of God—some sign, some revelation, some inward immanence—would be a consolation, a bonus, a sneak peak at what lies in store for those who persevere. But to depend on such a consolation, to seek it out as evidence, seems dangerous. If I didn't find it, would I then reject the faith as false?

It's not as if I'm opposed to the idea. I don't avoid the occasion. During my high school years, my family attended several events that were part of the charismatic movement within the Catholic Church. The great focus of the movement, it seemed to me, was the Holy Spirit and Its power to enflame the hearts of the faithful, making them burn with zeal and love. At some services, charismatic priests would lay hands on those who wished it, praying for the Holy Spirit to descend upon them. Some of these people would drop to the ground as if stricken, then lie ramrod straight, their eyes fluttering about under closed lids, their mouths mumbling at lightning speed. We called it being "slain in the Spirit." My father and I both went under the hands; neither of us were slain. "That sort of thing just doesn't happen to Lickonas," I concluded.

෴෴෴

I MISSED OUT AGAIN when I visited Medjugorje—site of an alleged Marian apparition—with my mother during Christmas 1990. Mine was the only rosary in the family that didn't see its chain turn golden. Even the folks back home were affected—my brother, my grandfather. My dad's rosary went gold on his birthday, four months later. It wasn't exactly an experience of God, but whatever it was, I was not a part of it.

Our Medjugorje party included two Dominican nuns, Sister Angela and Sister Catherine Marie. Sister Angela was older, but both women seemed to have fulfilled Christ's command that we become like little children. They did not strike me as naïve or innocent about the world and its wisdom, but they seemed to have successfully put all that aside for something simpler and better. Except for one occasion, they were happy and serene, no matter what the circumstances.

That one occasion was a fifteen-decade rosary walk up the side of a steep, rocky hill adorned with bronze reliefs of the stations of the cross. To my memory, it was just the three of us. At one point, Sister Angela looked up at the sun, which some people said had behaved strangely in the sky, perhaps dancing as it did at Fatima. Her serene countenance cracked, and out slipped a bit of genuine childish desire. She called to the sun, "Come on, dance!" She had come all this way; so many things had been reported. She had given God her life. I did not think she was asking for a reward, but a consolation. The sun stayed put. Sister Angela smiled and gently chided herself. "I do see miracles," she said to me. "Every day at Mass."

I didn't get any signs at Medjugorje either. But I was happy. I was happy because I was reading G. K. Chesterton's little book on St. Francis, where religion was presented as "a thing like a love affair" (G. K. Chesterton, *St. Francis of Assisi* [New York: Image Books, 2001], 8). The saint was my consolation. Reading about his insanely happy life amid hardship and poverty and suffering was my vicarious experience of God, only it didn't feel vicarious. My faith was bolstered by Francis's faith. The second leg of our pilgrimage took us to Rome and included a day trip to Assisi. There, amid the frescoes on the low, barrel-vaulted walls of the lower basilica, I experienced the keenest welling up of pure, sweet sentiment I have ever known. *Of course I will be a priest*, I thought. *A Franciscan. What could possibly be better than this?*

SWEET AS IT WAS, it didn't last. And I hesitate to call it an experience of God. I know I have never experienced God the way

Chesterton said Francis did—His being and love illuminated by all creation. The closest I get to that is when I actually get close to Him: when I witness the miracle of transubstantiation Sister Angela alluded to and then receive His body into mine. And there are times after confession that are similar. I am conscious that He has intervened in my life, and I am capable of genuine gratitude. Out of that gratitude comes love. Sometimes, that love is a hunger, the pang of the heart's true desire. I don't know if I have had the experience of God, but I know I have felt the lack where that experience should be, and that is a real start.

_ɹ͡ɒ ɹ͡ɒ ɹ͡ɒ ɹ͡ɒ ɹ͡ɒ_

et in arcadia ego

THOMAS AQUINAS COLLEGE, TAC, is a young school, founded in 1971. When, twenty years later, I arrived at its rather bucolic campus in the live oak-strewn hills halfway between Santa Paula and Ojai, it appeared less grand than it does today. Now, the construction of the college is well on its way to completion, with a high-ceilinged showpiece library, a science building, and a number of new dorms. Then, it was still molting, still shedding the dun-colored mobile units that made up its early physical structure in favor of the white stucco that now covers much of the campus.

Saint Joseph's Commons was finished; its main space served as cafeteria, lecture/concert hall, and dance floor, where I lurched my way through a smattering of swings and waltzes and sat out the Landler and Virginia Reel. The rest of the Commons housed the mailroom, bookstore, chapel, music room, student lounge/movie theater, and library. St. Augustine's Hall, its ten classrooms easily accommodating the school's roughly two hundred students, had recently been completed. And there were two permanent dorms: St. Katherine's for the girls and St. Bernard's for the boys. Visitation was prohibited—no boys in girls' dorms and vice versa—and punishable by expulsion. So was drinking on campus. Like the school's dress code and curfew, these rules were set in place to preserve the common good and aid in the pursuit of the scholarly life. Nobody complained much; we knew the rules going in. And mostly, we obeyed—especially when it came to visitation and drinking.

But the rest of the dorms, the dorms in which I spent my four happy undergraduate years, were gloriously low-rent mobile units, their paper-thin walls covered by wood paneling, their common areas furnished with gorgeous thrift-store relics from the seventies. One particularly florid orange sectional we dubbed the Bed of Sin, if only because of its salacious appearance against the pale, burnt-popcorn paneling. Francis, an English Catholic out of Stonyhurst who became my best friend freshman year, had mistaken his new digs for generator sheds as he first ascended the long, curving drive around the lower pond. No TVs were permitted, and after curfew, a single telephone booth served as our line to the world outside.

If it sounds oppressive, it wasn't. I loved the college, and not the way a captive may begin to love his captor. I spent two summers on campus working for the admissions office, and it would be easy, even now, to slip into a well-rehearsed rhapsody over the school's virtues. It would be equally easy to poke fun at its quirks, to draw a knowing smile and nod of the head from anyone who was there and lived it with me. But I will let the Bed of Sin suffice for the quirks, and for virtues, I will say only that TAC is a classically modeled Great Books school: no textbooks, no lectures, just original texts and discussion. If seminars sometimes veered toward monologues, and if the Great Books occasionally became the Great Handouts, it was still wonderful—a revelatory introduction to the life of the mind.

WHAT I WILL TRY TO CONVEY is some notion of the place's effect on my faith, the way the multihued tapestry of Catholicism unfolded before me. To begin with, though there were non-Catholics among the students and tutors, the college provided my first experience of a Catholic community. In Philip Roth's novel *Portnoy's Complaint*, Alexander Portnoy flees a disastrous tryst in Greece by flying to Tel Aviv. He recounts that "what gave my entire sojourn the air of the preposterous was one simple but wholly (to me) implausible fact: I am in a Jewish country. In this country, everybody is Jewish" (Philip Roth, *Portnoy's Complaint* [New York: Random House, 1969], 253). I read those words several years after graduation, but they resonated. Tucked into its little hollow amid the hills, TAC was not unlike a separate country, one that was almost entirely Catholic. I had been in public school all my life; once outside my home, my religion had been a largely solitary experience. Now here I was, surrounded by my own kind. Amazing. A body could exhale, unclench a bit. In class, you weren't supposed to argue from premises that assumed the truth of the faith. But out of class, a webbing of shared beliefs made for a comfortable hammock. There was sin, of course, but we called it sin when we recognized it, and at our best, we exhorted one another with the sort of charity that Paul prescribes.

I discovered that the faith has an intellectual tradition. In freshman theology class, I read the Bible in its entirety for the first time. Sophomore year, it was St. Augustine—*On Nature and Grace, On Grace and Free Will, The Predestination of the Saints, The City of God*—with St. Athanasius and St. Anselm thrown in. Then two years spent thrashing out some of the questions from St. Thomas Aquinas's *Summa Theologica*. I learned that, far from being a crutch for the weak-minded, the faith was something that had been affirmed by wise men with a love for the truth.

Outside of class, I began attending one of the three Masses offered daily in the chapel, though I never did make it to rosary and compline. The Mass followed the same form as the Masses I knew growing up, but except for the readings and the homily, the priest and the congregation spoke in Latin, which I had never heard before outside of "Adeste Fideles." I wasn't long in picking it up, though, and I thrilled to the Sunday intonation of the Latin Our Father: *Pater Noster, qui est in caelis . . .* the whole congregation booming along. My fellow churchgoers were my fellow students. I was one of the faithful, in a way I had never been before. I attended Eucharistic Adoration, kneeling in silence before the consecrated Host in the gold monstrance on the altar. And after hearing a general invitation from Father Steckler, I decided to confess for the first time in six years.

I APPROACHED FATHER and asked for an appointment. He grinned slyly, his thin lips curling inward to expose powerful rows of teeth, and gave me Saturday morning at eight o'clock. Innocent that I was, I didn't wonder why that particular time slot should be free. And inevitably, Joseph, a junior who had taken a shine to me, picked the preceding Friday to relieve me of that innocence.

Though I had drunk alcohol a few times in high school, I was no drinker. I learned to drink at TAC, and I use the word *learned* with some care—there was a real aspect of education to it. Formally, that translated to a few evenings spent eating and drinking with tutors in their homes. Once, we freshmen took turns stumbling over attempts at description—is that dried grass in my Sauvignon Blanc?—and marveling at our masters' palates. Less formally, it meant on-campus formal dinners and parties where students drank and tutors supervised, rare exceptions to the on-campus alcohol policy. (The tutors watched over us, trying to make sure we stayed within the Scholastic limit of *ad hilaritatem*—to the point of hilarity.)

Even on those nights when we fled campus to drink at the beach, or by the cattle gate on a nearby hilltop, or under the highway overpass just off school grounds known affectionately as The Pit, there remained a general sense that we were doing this to relax and enjoy life, not to get wasted or laid. There was still shame in overindulgence, as I learned during that first outing with Joseph. Under his mischievous care, I was introduced to the pleasures of Wild Turkey bourbon. Today, Joseph is one of my dearest friends, and I am a great fan of Wild Turkey, but that night did not end well. A classmate stood above me as I hugged the toilet. "How you feeling there? Not too good, eh?" I wanted to kill him, but I stayed on the floor.

Still, I was a great one for duty, and I was scheduled to see a priest in the morning to confess my sins. I set my alarm, and managed to haul myself out of bed at 7:45. I made it to Father's study, peeled my tongue off the roof of my mouth and staggered down my list of offenses, starting with the previous evening's drunkenness. Father nodded and muttered, "Excellent, excellent," after each entry, as if delighted by this account of my multitudinous failings.

Later, I worked up the courage for a general confession, which Father recommended to people who'd been away from the sacrament. Father ran down a long list of sins; if I had committed one, I said, "Yes." If not, "No." Queries like "Any murder?" sparked a mild interest—*Imagine that: me, a murderer.* But others—"Any bestiality?"—were simply embarrassing, even if I *could* answer, "No." How could he ask that in the same tone he used for asking if I'd ever stolen anything?

A little lesson in the monotony of sin; I wasn't about to shock or surprise him. I began seeing Father every week for spiritual direction. Mostly that meant confessing my sins, but that was enough to create a new sensitivity for the soul and its care.

TAC WAS A GOOD PLACE FOR ME. It was not a new Eden. A life lived in common will help to uncover divisions that might have been invisible from afar. I learned that in some circles, I would be regarded as a liberal Catholic. For the first time, I heard criticisms of the *Novus Ordo* Mass, the rite instituted after the Second Vatican Council. It was, in some people's estimation, an objectively inferior form of worship when compared to the old Tridentine rite. Others argued that it was at least pedagogically inferior, diverting emphasis away from Christ's sacrifice, so powerfully expressed in the Host. I learned about *sedevacantes*, the idea that the Chair of Peter was empty, that the current pope was not really the pope.

None of this had anything to do with the college's mission to introduce people to the life of the mind in the light of Catholic revelation. You didn't find tutors debating these questions, and the school was not a refugee camp for the disgruntled faithful. A well-wisher warned one freshman, "I hope that you don't lose your faith at that *Novus Ordo* school." I had come to a place that most people I knew would see as anachronistic and backward, only to find that others viewed it as modern and flawed, the best they could do in a fallen world.

ᴐᴐᴐᴐᴐ

triddywackers, tinkerers, and the roar of the crowd

I SHOULD HAVE BEEN A BETTER STUDENT at college. I should have spent more time with Aristotle's *Posterior Analytics*, more time with my Latin, more time with Plato's dialogues. I should have avoided extracurricular debates about the alarming state of the church; that wasn't why I had come to California. But I was eighteen, and the world was new: here were kids who had been homeschooled until the day they left for college. Here were girls who wore small lace veils atop their heads when they entered the chapel, in keeping with Paul's admonition in his letter to the Corinthians. And here were these scintillating questions about the Mass.

Aristotle: "It is evident, then, that not everything demonstrable can be defined. What then? Can everything definable be demonstrated, or not?" How could that compete with tales of how the new Mass had been born amid a storm of controversy, dark dealing, and Protestant midwifery during the Second

Vatican Council? What was Latin vocabulary compared to the *Ottaviani Intervention*, the 1969 letter from two cardinals to Pope Paul VI decrying the institution of the *Novus Ordo*?

I mostly heard from proponents of the Tridentine rite—Triddywackers, as my bourbon-sharing friend Joseph self-identifies. They felt marginalized. In the encyclical *Ecclesia Dei*, Pope John Paul II had stated that the Tridentine rite should be made available to the faithful, but they were forever having to search for the approved Indult Mass actually provided by a given diocese. The *Novus Ordo* Catholics did not seem eager to join the debate, except for one normally taciturn student who argued with surprising emotion, "The current order of Mass was instituted for a reason. Things weren't perfect in the old days. A lot of times, people would say their rosaries during Mass instead of paying attention, because it was so hard to follow."

I believed him. Growing up, I noticed that at the beginning of Mass, my maternal grandmother would take out her rosary beads, wrap them tightly around her hand, and recite the prayers in silence. I thought this odd. Mom had told me in somber tones that I should never look toward the back of the church during Mass, never turn my back on the priest. I should pay attention to his celebration of the liturgy. Was my grandmother paying attention to the Mass or her rosary? Apparently, the order of Mass had changed, but she hadn't.

THAT SAME YEAR, at a Catholic book sale on campus, I bought a prayer guide entitled *Devotions for Holy Communion.* I liked the pious, old-timey illustrations, the meditations from the saints, the crinkly onion-skin pages. The book had an ancient air, and offered what I took to be an antique piece of advice: it opened by saying that while the Mass was a communal prayer and should be attended to by the faithful, sometimes it might be helpful to read books like this one instead. The tacit admission seemed to be that the Tridentine rite was indeed hard to follow, especially if you had one of those missals with a dozen ribbons of various colors to lead you through the prayers. There were sacred mysteries to be celebrated, but perhaps the celebration of those mysteries was for some too mysterious, too obscure, to engage the soul properly.

Or perhaps people didn't know their liturgical Latin and were therefore shut out of the proceedings, especially if they were illiterate. For such as these, the rise of the Mass in the vernacular, the Mass that soon became synonymous with the *Novus Ordo,* may have been a great blessing. But it also gave rise to the priest-tinkerer, the man who makes the Mass his own. It's so much easier to ad-lib in your native tongue.

ৡৡৡৡৡ

FATHER FRANK, A FORMER PASTOR at St. Mary's back in Cortland, was a tinkerer. Father Frank was a showman. Every year, he directed a Passion Play—using young people—that toured upstate New York. Two of those years, I was Jesus, my thirteen- and fourteen-year-old self beaten, crowned with thorns, and crucified to wonderful effect. As he drove us to rehearsal, he played the soundtrack to *Evita*; now and then, I still find myself singing little bits of the lyrics.

That showman quality came out in the way he said Mass. Normally, the elevation of the Host and chalice follows after the consecration of each—a moment for the faithful to behold their God made present in the Eucharist. But Father Frank performed the elevation and consecration simultaneously. He didn't want your head bowed down during the miracle of transubstantiation; he wanted eyes front and center. I will never forget the slow pan he used to perform with the chalice, bearing it slowly from right to left as he held it aloft, stared out at the congregation, and said the words: ". . . and whenever you do this . . . you do it always . . . in remembrance . . . of me."

But of course, that's not quite it. The order of Mass reads, "Do this in memory of me." The Gospel of Luke has it as, "Do this in remembrance of me." In either case, it's a command. In Father Frank's version, it's a pronouncement, a reminder: "Whenever you do this . . ."

Years later, I heard a priest give a homily in which he recalled hearing in seminary that it is a mortal sin to change any of the words of the consecration. He cited this as an example of the bad old legalistic days in the church. In one sense, I see his point. Saying that anything is a mortal sin simply is, I think, simplistic, since the will must be informed and engaged for a sin to be mortal. But that's looking only at the sin's subjective effect on the soul—the culpability of the offender. Sin also has an objective character, and to say that such an act constitutes a grievous offense against God—the exterior condition for serious sin—seems entirely appropriate. My inner punk wanted to shake him and say, "Dude, it's the words of Jesus. At the Last Supper. Don't mess around."

I do not wish to speculate as to whether Father Frank's tinkering rendered his consecrations invalid, nor do I wish to speculate as to its effect on his soul. I merely cite it to help explain why a person might miss the Latin. Most often, tinkering creates a distraction, and it hits me like a spiritual sucker-punch. I get my one hour to worship God in the church, and suddenly I'm wincing at some novel rendering of "Behold the Lamb of God, who takes away the sin of the world."

THE TRIDENTINE CROWD also has my sympathy when it decries the subordination of the sacrificial aspect of the Mass for the sake of the communal aspect—the altar of unbloody sacrifice versus the table of the Last Supper. I once talked to an architect who had designed a church in the round, one that allowed parishioners to gaze upon one another across the sunken sanctuary. He told me that people had gotten tired of sitting and looking in the same direction as if they were on an airplane. For me, that raised the question of what they were looking at; the priest, after all, is not a supernatural flight attendant, demonstrating the salvation equipment before an audience numb with familiarity. It raised the question of whether the Mass ought to direct our attention toward one another or toward something that unites us in the worship of something greater than ourselves, something divine.

I tend toward the sacrificial side of things—the Body given up for me, the Blood shed for my sake. I regard the redemption of sinful man (me) so that he may enter into the life of God to be the chief point of Christianity. The sacrifice represented in the Mass made that redemption possible. And it is the sacrifice that gives meaning to the meal we gather to share, because it is through the sacrifice that we get the Body broken for us, the Blood poured out on our behalf. I don't gather with my fellow Catholics for the sake of gathering; I gather to be united to Christ. I am also united to my neighbor, but only because we are both members of His Mystical Body.

That's not to say I squirm when some aspects of the Mass emphasize that unity. I like that the congregation joins in some of the prayers—the Confiteor, the Gloria, the Creed, the Our Father. The community is speaking with one voice in a way that one voice might not make clear. As second semester of freshman year bumped along, a student wrote an essay that compared the "garbled drone" of the faithful during a *Novus Ordo* Mass to the roaring of the angry crowds on Good Friday. I thought his claim extreme. The drone may be less than harmonious, less than beautiful, but I think there is value in it. There are times when the priest acts and speaks as only he can, and those times must be preserved inviolate. But I wouldn't want him to shoulder the entire liturgical burden. I might get to feeling as if I had nothing to do with it, as if it was not "our sacrifice of praise" that was being offered, but only the priest's. This would work on a lurking belief that spiritual matters are the business of spiritual men—men who make holiness their business, as it were.

Such an attitude would play on my spiritual sloth. I might drift, not into the pious recitation of the rosary, but into my own reverie. Lord knows, even with the Mass in English, distraction is a familiar bugbear for me. As a teenager, I was plagued with impure thoughts during the liturgy. (I regarded that kind of temptation without occasion as a powerful argument for the existence of the devil.) To counter it, I imagined the evil phantasm as occupying the space between my skull and my brain, the organ having contracted as it ceased contemplating its proper object. I then pictured my brain swelling with renewed vigor and attention, spattering the phantasm against the inside of my skull, leaving flesh-toned splotches of color as it slid down and away.

Now, I contend with less obvious monsters, thoughts not evil in themselves, but out of place during worship. I am not alone in this. My father once admitted that he was having a terrible time with distraction during Mass. It had gotten to the point where he sometimes missed the consecration. He asked for advice. I suggested kneeling without the kneeler, letting the pain of hard wood against unprotected knees alert him to the business at hand.

ฅฅฅฅฅ

AFTER FRESHMAN YEAR, the Mass controversy died down. I attended a few Tridentine Masses, but was not won over. It was not my Mass. I was not born until after the change, and had not grown up in some community of holdouts. Also, I indulged in a certain populist pride—the *Novus Ordo* was the Mass said the world over, the Mass of the struggling, heaving church on earth. I did not want to be in the company of the remnant of a remnant, one of the few who supposedly knew better than the rest. "If it's good enough for the pope," I thought, "it's good enough for me."

I still think that, but on December 21 of 2003, I attended the Tridentine Mass marking the fiftieth anniversary of the ordination of Father Harry Neely. The Mass was celebrated in the Immaculata Church at the University of San Diego, with a full choir and about forty priests in attendance. The cavernous church, all plaster-white and Marian blue, was packed; my family and I ended up sitting behind the altar. The next two hours made a tremendous assault upon my supposed indifference to the rite. Everything worked on me—the soaring and ancient music from the full choir in the loft, the ornate vestments, the shifting rainbows of light through the stained-glass windows, the massive silence of the throng, the evident holiness of Father Neely.

But most of all, I delighted in the words of the Mass, the translated text of which I struggled to read as I held my sleeping two-year-old daughter. The words of the priest before proclaiming the Gospel: "Cleanse my heart and my lips, O Almighty God, Who cleansed the lips of the Prophet Isaiah with a burning coal. In Your gracious mercy deign so to purify me that I may worthily proclaim Your holy Gospel. Through Christ our Lord. Amen." His words as he prepares the incense for the offertory: "Let my prayer, O Lord, come like incense before You; the lifting up of my hands, like the evening sacrifice. O Lord, set a watch before my mouth, a guard at the door of my lips. Let not my heart incline to the evil of engaging in deeds of wickedness." The burning coal, the evening sacrifice, the guard at the door of my lips—the Mass was poetry, its wonderful imagery recalling my senses to worship.

I realized that it was foolish to avoid the Tridentine rite simply because I suspected my fellow attendees of feeling superior. I found the Mass glorious, vivid and vivifying, even transcendent. Granted, the circumstances were ideal: a High Mass in a beautiful place, honoring a priest I admired. But something else was different, something interior. For the first time, I had appreciated the old Mass not for what it avoided, but for what it offered.

ᕉᕉᕉᕉᕉ

lent and its discontents

TO ME, THOMAS AQUINAS COLLEGE was a spiritual greenhouse, a place where religious flora, imported from all sorts of environs, could flourish in a protective Catholic atmosphere. There, I encountered practices, beliefs, and traditions that had withered away in the more arid, post–Vatican II climes of my upbringing. Some never lost the whiff of antiquity—the veneration of saints' relics, for example—but others, such as Eucharistic Adoration, took firm root in my soul. Small wonder that my thoughts often drift back to those years; they bear something of the character of a conversion. In that place, I had found new zeal for the faith.

When Lent of freshman year arrived, I was ready to turn that zeal toward self-denial. I had always taken Lent seriously enough to be frustrated with my fellow public-school Catholics when they left school on Ash Wednesday just to get out of school, indifferent to the smudged black cross they received on their forehead while at Mass. But I had never really denied myself for Christ's sake. Most years, I gave up candy, but I certainly didn't love candy enough to really miss it. This year, I would partake of a true fast. My friend Francis and I went on a bread and oatmeal diet—four slices of Orowheat Honey Wheat Berry bread for breakfast, four slices for lunch, and a bowl of oatmeal for dinner. Only water to drink. At midnight on Saturday, as the "little Easter" of Sunday began, we would call the local Domino's Pizza. Francis, a man of enormous stature and appetite, once put away two large pizzas during our celebratory binge. I was stuffed after one.

Those who discussed their chosen penances—and a bunch of us did—fell into three groups. Some were purists who didn't take Sundays off. My group called them rigorists and told them to count the days from Ash Wednesday to Easter. The only way to get the traditional forty days of Lent was by leaving Sundays out. Others started their Sunday celebration after the Vigil Mass late Saturday afternoon, giving them all Saturday night to indulge. They argued that if the Vigil Mass fulfilled your Sunday Mass obligation, then Sunday was underway, liturgically speaking. Wasn't Lent over after the Vigil on Holy Saturday? I couldn't bring myself to join them, but I had no real argument to offer. I, after all, allowed myself St. Patrick's Day to celebrate, along with the Solemnity of St. Joseph and the Feast of the Annunciation. According to one of the school's more traditional souls, I was right in thinking that penance was not to be observed during the latter two feasts, but St. Paddy's was my own invention.

Starting sophomore year, I gave up alcohol. By then, it was something I loved enough to miss. I also tried an early-morning regimen of push-ups, sit-ups, and jogging alongside the highway that led to campus, a hilly, winding, mile-long circuit. This was splendid penance. I detested exercise outside of athletic games, gagged on the sulfuric smell from a nearby mountain as it mixed with the hot exhaust of passing cars, and faltered daily on the uphill return to campus. A pulled hamstring during a soccer game put an end to my suffering. I was grateful to be hobbled.

Those attempts at mortification were not useless; they were honest efforts toward letting my faith have an impact on my daily life. But while the flesh was willing, the spirit was weak. Mine were feats of endurance, not charity. It showed in the way I talked about them with friends, not exactly flaunting them in public to show my holiness, but still eager for my intimates to know my struggles. "Gosh, this Lent thing is tough, no?" I was gutting it out, sucking it up, struggling toward the relief of Easter, when I would offer Christ my sacrifice-scrubbed soul.

MY SPIRIT WAS (IS) PELAGIAN. Among other things, Pelagius argued that the first move in the romance between God and man was man's to make. Sophomore year, I read as St. Augustine carefully dismantled Pelagius's claim that man's will can avail him anything without the grace of God. I read, as if for the first time, Paul's rhetorical question, "What have you that you did not receive?" (1 Corinthians 4:7). Life is a gift. Redemption is a gift. Faith is a gift. As I jogged along, gasping for wind, I repeated to myself, "What will you do for Christ, who has done all things for you?" I wanted to give something back, namely, the cramp in my side and the ache in my legs. But if Christ had done all, what could I do? The question of grace and free will is a thorny one, but I know my own case.

I know that in times of suffering, self-imposed or otherwise, I look first to myself. God is the backup, to be called upon when I find myself insufficient.

Lent 1999 showed the folly of that notion. Ash Wednesday came and went amid a morass of work-related troubles. I write for the *San Diego Reader*, a weekly newspaper. It's a great job, and I get to work at home and set my own schedule. But for many of my stories, I don't get paid until I actually turn something in, and it takes a measure of self-discipline to keep self-imposed deadlines from sliding further down the calendar. I was up against it.

I told myself I would get to Lent when I got out of the swamp. I had intended to take up daily spiritual reading from the Liturgy of the Hours, but wasn't sure how it was done. The book had more of those multicolored ribbons to lead you from place to place, and I didn't know how to use them. I gave up TV as a sort of stopgap measure until I found someone to teach me.

The swamp thickened, and when my parents flew out from New York to visit for a week, a black mood settled over me. I was touchy, frustrated, and sulky—thoroughly unpleasant company. My mother gently reminded me of St. John of the Cross's exhortation: "One prayer of thanksgiving when things go badly is worth a thousand when things go well." She encouraged me to praise the Lord at all times. I responded with impatience, even anger. Why was it hard to hear a suggestion from a parent whose love was unquestioned, a suggestion that I seek help from the surest source? Why did I hold on to my suffering, trying to grit my teeth and pull myself out?

Pride, pride of a masculine sort. Before daily prayer was a true habit for my father, my mother could always tell when he hadn't prayed. He was grouchy and irritable. He didn't handle the frequently intense stress of his work nearly as well. The same was true for my brother. By Easter 1999, Mark was a father twice over, with a master's degree in theology and a burning desire to break into the movie business. Meanwhile, he was trying to swallow his frustration with his job teaching Catholic high school. If he didn't pray, he said, he had a hard time swallowing.

Now it was my turn. "It's important for men to pray," said Mom. "To submit themselves to Christ." Everyone must bend his or her will, but this desire to clean up one's own spiritual mess seems a more masculine failing. From a distance, the danger is easy to see: "It's my problem, I'll deal with it," leading to, "It's my soul, I'll sanctify it." No, you won't.

The problem is maintaining enough distance to keep that in mind. While in college, I read about a vision St. Jerome had of the child Jesus. Jesus asked Jerome why he hadn't given Him everything. Jerome was mystified. "Lord," he protested, "I have devoted my life to your service. I have given you all my works, all my love, all my praise, everything." "No," Jesus replied, "You haven't given me your sins." Give it over, offer it up. Be clay. Submit.

I have assented to this thought for some time, but I have not managed to send it over the gap between intellect and will. When I was confirmed at age fifteen, I took St. John the Baptist as my confirmation saint. "A voice crying out in the wilderness," I thought, full of adolescent pride. I would preach to my generation, lead them back to the faith they had never really known. By Lent of 2003, a little older and a little more humble—if only as a result of years of sin and failure to do much crying out—I found myself dwelling more on another of the Baptist's lines: "He must increase, but I must decrease" (John 3:30).

I began to dread the inevitable question from the priest at the holy season's end: "Have you drawn closer to Christ these past forty days?" Has He increased; have you decreased? Do you think of His supreme sacrifice every time you find yourself thirsting for a self-denied Manhattan cocktail? Have you even been able to explain to your curious son why it is good to give things up for Lent?

֍֍֍֍֍

THESE ARE NOT DECREASING TIMES. Not only is man often seen as the measure of all things, each individual man often sees *himself* as the measure of all things. The very existence of the magisterium implies that people need to be taught and formed, and yet the pope and the teaching church are ignored on this, that, and the other as a matter of course. I try to be obedient, but even so, I am hardly free of my inflated self. When Hamlet declares, "What a piece of work is man, how noble in reason, how infinite in faculties; in form and moving, how express and admirable; in action, how like an angel; in apprehension, how like a god!" (William Shakespeare, "Hamlet," in *The Riverside Shakespeare* [Boston: Houghton Mifflin, 1974], 2.2.1350–53, p. 1156), I am tempted to nod in recognition, or at least to claim that I am basically a good person.

But Hamlet knew better: "I am myself indifferent honest, but yet I could accuse me of such things that it were better my mother had not borne me. I am very proud, revengeful, ambitious, with more offenses at my beck than I have thoughts to put them in, imagination to give them shape, or time to act them in" (ibid., 3.1.1777–1781, p. 1161). The trouble is that I do not have eyes to see these offenses. I cannot imagine saying with the psalmist, "My sin is ever before me" (Psalm 51:3). What sin?

Pick one, Matthew, pick an easy one—say, complaining—and try to give it up. Try to control your tongue (to say nothing of your other members). Your first reaction may be to dismiss complaint as hardly any sin at all. Granted, it is not mortal. But is it not pride? Does it not spring from the supposition that you are due better than what you have received, you who have been given life and redemption by no merit of your own? Is it not ingratitude? Are you not grumbling after your fleshpots even as you are fed manna from heaven?

Complaint is common currency, the stuff of small talk: "Let me tell you about my day . . ." It's a mouse of a sin, nibbling at the edges of the soul—not as serious as speaking ill of others, or snapping at someone. Very well, should it not therefore be easier to avoid? So go ahead; try to stop it. You say you do it without thinking, that you're barely even conscious of it? That just means it's habitual, practically second nature, and therefore that much harder to root out.

So I started concentrating on avoiding the near occasion of complaint. I started catching myself just after complaining, wincing at the twinge of guilt. Then I started catching myself before complaining, which meant I started feeling good about my success. I grew complacent, lost vigilance, and started backsliding. After a while, I got tired of the effort. Surely I was blowing this out of proportion, expending way too much effort on such a minor offense. Why obsess about complaining? Why obsess about sin?

I know there is danger in dwelling overmuch on man's wretchedness. Paul says, "where sin increased, grace increased all the more" (Romans 5:20). Shouldn't I focus on grace, on gratitude and love? Perhaps. I know that the grace of Christ will have to be the ultimate cause of my decreasing; I haven't forgotten my Augustine. But it helps to keep in mind those aspects of the self that must decrease if He is to increase. It helps to remember that I am a sinner, that "if we say we have no sin, we deceive ourselves, and the truth is not in us" (1 John 1:8). It is so easy to forget.

ᴐᴐᴐᴐᴐ

swimming with scapulars

IF RELICS NEVER CAPTURED MY INTEREST and Adoration became a real part of my everyday faith, the scapular hovered somewhere in between. It never quite lost its aura of ancient mystery, but neither was I comfortable consigning it to the dim storehouse of faded tradition. I first encountered it on my desk freshman year, along with a note from Joseph saying that he heard I hadn't been "bagged" yet. (The woolen squares at the end of the strings reminded him of teabags.) He urged me to take up the sacramental, saying something along the lines of "every little bit of grace helps."

I didn't feel bullied—no mean feat in matters of spiritual counsel—in part because Joseph and I were already friends. I visited Father Steckler (per Joseph's instructions), received a blessing, and was enrolled in the scapular. After that, I didn't think much about it, except to wonder whether I ought to leave it on in the shower. When I lost it in the ocean over Christmas break, I made no effort to get another.

And why should I have made an effort? I hadn't done anything differently while wearing it, hadn't said any special prayers or cultivated any particular devotion. I was not ready to believe that a scapular could serve as a sort of grace magnet, acting independently from my own efforts. I was fixed in the rather contradictory notion that I had to do something in order to attain grace. Augustine had taught me that if grace is earned, then it's not grace—not a free gift but a just reward. But I didn't think of that at the time. And I was still suspicious of the scapular; it was too much like a talisman for my tastes. The promise of salvation to the wearer sounded too close to superstition.

Before I lost my scapular, I tried to get my brother to take it up, arguing, "Why wouldn't you want to?" This was the very spiritual bullying I had been glad to avoid, akin to asking, "Why wouldn't you want to join me in praying fifteen decades of the rosary daily? Don't you love our Lady?" No doubt stung by my question, Mark responded, "I'll stick to the sacraments, thank you." I didn't know how to answer him.

Had I thought of it, I could have pointed out that we both employed the sacramental of holy water, dipping our fingers into the font and crossing ourselves as we entered a church for Mass. This practice was easier to understand in its relation to the recipient's disposition: the water reminded us of our baptism; the sign of the cross, of our redemption. The memory was awakened, and hopefully, the will was touched. We were encouraged to be purified by repentance and to give thanks to our Redeemer. But holy water involved doing something. That comforted my Pelagian soul. Again, how could just wearing a thing provide spiritual benefit? It seemed so external.

A similar case: many of the girls at the college I attended—including my wife—developed an attachment to a little Marian-blue book of prayers entitled *The Pieta*. Besides prayers to Mary, the book included a list of promises from the Blessed Mother made to St. Dominic. Promise Number 8 read, "Those who will recite my rosary shall find during their life and at their death the light of God, the fullness of His grace, and shall share in the merits of the blessed." Now granted, many of the other promises included the condition that the rosary must be recited piously, and that souls must trust themselves to the Blessed Virgin through the rosary—a good will was needed. But what a promise, this Promise Number 8!

I read it again years later in a little book of rosary novenas to our Lady. There on the title page, I found both the *Nihil Obstat* and the *Imprimatur*, the signs that the book contained nothing contrary to the faith and was published with the permission of the Holy See or the Episcopal conference. I wasn't about to judge the church's use of the imprimatur, so I never bleated my hesitations. But there was in those promises something a little too material, something bordering on the exterior: "Say these prayers and you'll get to heaven," as opposed to, "Love Christ and you'll get to heaven."

PLEASE DON'T MISUNDERSTAND ME. I am no enemy of the exterior. I believe that matter matters to the spiritual life, to the point where God cares about what I do with my body in the marriage bed. Even before the Incarnation, God was asking the Jews to perform physical sacrifices—killing animals, sacrificing first fruits, cutting off the foreskin. What He wanted, He said, was contrite hearts, but He still asked for exterior acts. And then His son took flesh, and commanded us to eat His flesh and drink His blood. And Paul writes that the union of man and wife in matrimony, a union in which they become one flesh, is a great sign of the mysterious union of Christ and his church. But the sacraments have a scriptural basis. The church teaches that they were instituted by Christ. It is the *church*, however, which institutes sacramentals—rosaries, relics, scapulars—and it is the church that may abolish them.

But the church hasn't abolished scapulars. They weren't done away with, by Vatican II or anything else. Neither were indulgences—remission for the temporal punishment of sin, obtained, according to my *Catholic Encyclopedia*, from "the treasure of the merits of the saints, from Christ himself, or from His mother" (Reverend Peter M. J. Stravinskas, PhD, STD, ed. *Our Sunday Visitor's Catholic Encyclopedia* [Huntington: Our Sunday Visitor Publishing Division, 1991], 509). It sounds very old-fashioned, but there it is, still on the books. In the jubilee year of 2000, the pope issued a Bull of Indiction that decreed that the faithful might gain plenary indulgences for themselves and for the souls in purgatory by worthily performing a number of practices. The whole thing seemed odd enough to me to keep me from pursuing such indulgences, but my father jumped at the chance. The Bull limited a person to one indulgence per day, but I know he obtained as many as he could, applying them hopefully to a host of the deceased, including one man who had bitterly opposed him on the question of abortion.

Hearing about my father's efforts, I realized that the failure of indulgences or scapulars to make it into my personal deposit of faith did not make them any less valid. And the brown scapular I had worn, said my encyclopedia, was "the most indulgenced" of all scapulars. I turned to the *Catechism*. Sacramentals, it read, "signify effects, particularly of a spiritual nature, which are obtained through the intercession of the Church . . . by the Church's prayer, they prepare us to receive grace and dispose us to cooperate with it" (*Catechism of the Catholic Church* [Boston: Pauline Books & Media, 1994], 415).

That differs strongly from the notion of sacraments: "efficacious signs of grace . . . by which divine life is dispensed to us" (ibid., 293). But if the scapular could prepare me to receive grace and dispose me to cooperate with it, then the promise could be regarded as true without removing salvific grace from the realm of the sacraments. And wasn't it a sort of grace to be prepared and disposed? I decided my first idea, that of the scapular as grace magnet, was not quite as absurd as I had thought. My scapular attracted to me the intercessory prayer of the church. It sounded strange, but then, the unity of the Mystical Body of Christ had allowed my father to free the souls in purgatory by his prayers here on earth, and that sounded strange as well. I was humbled. Who was I to place a limit on the workings of grace?

A YEAR OR SO LATER, I noticed my father wearing a scapular. Then my brother. Finally, in 2002, I bought one for myself at a traveling Catholic book sale that had stopped at our parish. Or rather, I bought one and then exchanged it for another. The original was a tasteful little number with no more adornment than the cross of the crusaders. I had seen one that bore an image of St. Thérèse of Lisieux, a great favorite of mine because of her Little Way to sanctity. I had once lamented the idea that I would most likely never achieve greatness; greatness seemed beyond the scope of modern man, or at least modern me. Thérèse had shown me that greatness was not necessary. But if Thérèse's way was small, her scapular was huge, a regular honker, the woolen equivalent of Mr. Evangelista's gigantic gold cross. The background behind Thérèse was not an unassuming brown, but a bold sky blue.

Then, as I drove away, I started to worry that Thérèse would be disappointed that I had eschewed her image just because it was too big. "You're asking me for all this help," she would scold, "and yet you're embarrassed of me?" Shame of that kind is such a pathetic sin; I had to go for the big honker if I was ever to raise my voice to her again. I turned around.

Our Lady's scapular promise—the one about the wearer not suffering eternal fire—is stitched on the back square of this one. The back square is particularly visible, as it is forever poking out from above the back of my T-shirt. "What," I wondered as a chiropractor began fiddling with my crimped neck recently, "is this lady thinking? She's got to be reading the thing." God forgive me, I took it off, half because I didn't want it to be in her way, half because I didn't want to try to explain it—or worse, not be given a chance to explain it. Like plenary indulgences, scapulars to me are not the sort of thing you want to lead with when you're presenting the faith. Much more than, say, Marian devotion, they seem quirky, easy to shrug off as the indefensible superstitions of a peasant religion. Better to start with fallen nature, humanity's need for redemption, the love of God.

I shouldn't have presumed. As I left her office, she reminded me not to forget my scapular. She had known what it was all along, and if so, didn't she also know why I had taken it off?

I could have been the quietest of witnesses, but I was afraid of what she'd think.

Not long after, I had another opportunity, and I would like to be able to tell the happy story of how I was finally dragged kicking and screaming out of my little Catholic womb and forced to witness to another soul, only to find myself filled with the Spirit of truth. A contractor—whose talk revealed that his grandmother, at least, was Catholic—asked me about my scapular. Yes, it would be nice to relate such a story, but alas.

I knew I had to say something; the man asked, after all. I was in a bad way. I had stepped outside to avoid losing my temper with my children, but I tried to recover. I resolved to try my best to sound like my friend Kathy when she related to my pagan mother-in-law, with heartbreaking sincerity, the story of Juan Diego and Our Lady of Guadalupe. When she told it, it was all there, recounted in tones as relaxed and historical as a vacation slideshow, right down to the roses growing out of place and out of season.

Hearing it so told was touching. It also made me deeply uncomfortable. Why? The apparition has been confirmed. The story, even if gussied up with pious accretions, may be affirmed with confidence by the faithful. Why should I be antsy around declarations of a faith that I tell myself I would die for? Why should the concrete stories of saints, the very things that reassure me in moments of doubt, seem so ridiculous when placed before unbelievers?

So there was my chance to lay it out, straight and true. I wobbled. When I spoke, I found myself distancing myself from the thing: "Well, the story goes . . ." But after years of wearing it, I still didn't know the full story. I hadn't consulted my encyclopedia or my *Catechism*; all I knew was our Lady's promise. It would have sounded better if I had been able to say, "Pious tradition holds that in 1251, our Lady appeared to St. Simon Stock, a member of the Carmelite order. She told him that those who wore the Carmelite scapular would enjoy her special protection, and would not suffer eternal fire. It's a sacramental—like holy water. It can dispose a soul to receive grace." But all I could manage was, "Well, the story goes . . ." My embarrassment showed; I knew that my account left the scapular looking like a magic necklace that would save you from hell—exactly what I didn't want.

My attempt may not have been a total loss, however. At the very least, my contractor may have been interested to find this young man, who could discuss the merits of Nine

Inch Nails, believed the same sorts of things as his pious old grandmother. And at the *very* least, my mention of death and hell gave him an oblique reminder of mortality. He gave me a funny look. "You been driving too fast lately?" I bumbled into my response: "No, but you never know when the Lord's gonna take you."

PART II

∽∽∽∽∽

AT HOME

∽∽∽∽∽

ɷ ɷ ɷ ɷ ɷ

deirdre

BESIDES BOURBON AND THE SCAPULAR, Joseph also introduced me to Catholic literature—or rather, literature written by Catholic authors. He didn't put it so grandly, of course. What he said was that he had discovered a great novel called *Love in the Ruins*, written by a guy named Walker Percy. I borrowed his copy, and fell completely in love. I had heard Percy speak, shortly before his death, at my brother's graduation from Notre Dame in 1989. But he didn't mean anything to me until I read him. Joseph and I took endless delight in *Love*'s lustful, knowing, bourbon-swilling hero, Dr. Tom More. He favored Early Times instead of Wild Turkey, but we forgave him that.

Over the next couple of years, I read all the Percy I could find, even digging into *The Message in a Bottle*, his text on symbol theory. Percy, like his fictional alter ego More, was a diagnostician, searching for the dis-ease at the heart of modern man. He didn't skewer the objects of his satire so much as he pinned them to a board for closer study.

When I had finished, I read him again. Eventually, the stars faded from my eyes, and I saw some of his weaknesses. In places, he seemed too much of a philosopher, not enough of a novelist. I stopped reading him for years. But his words had already sunk deep into me, taking up residence in my long-term memory. They still bubble up in all sorts of situations, little moments of *a-ha* recognition.

Evelyn Waugh was another discovery. I had classmates who couldn't believe I had never read *Brideshead Revisited*, perhaps the most overtly Catholic of Waugh's novels. Here again, Joseph provided my introduction. I started with Waugh's satire—*Decline and Fall, Vile Bodies, A Handful of Dust*. Seemingly without effort, Waugh achieved the same immediate effect on me as Camus. Tony Last's nightmarish fate in *A Handful of Dust* had twisted my guts and made me queasy with horror. By the time I got to *Brideshead*, I was a disciple. Imagine, then, the shadow cast by this passage from the novel's opening: "I was aghast to realize that something within me, long sickening, had quietly died, and felt as a husband might feel, who, in the fourth year of his marriage, suddenly knew that he had no longer any desire, or tenderness, or esteem, for a once-beloved wife; no pleasure in her company, no wish to please, no curiosity about anything she might ever do or say or think; no hope of setting things right, no self-reproach for the disaster" (Evelyn Waugh, *Brideshead Revisited* [London: Chapman & Hall, 1964], 14). After reading that, I wondered if I would ever have the courage to marry, knowing that such a moment was possible.

BUT I DID GET MARRIED, to a girl I met freshman year. At first, she was a curiosity. A freshman like me, though older, she was dating Joseph, a junior. She was curious to me because I knew that Joseph was in love with someone else—Cecilia, the woman he would eventually marry. Cecilia and Joseph weren't together just then, in any sense. She was at another school and had pulled away from the relationship. But Joseph still loved her, and here he was, abandoning his Wisconsin earth-goddess for the more proximate joys of a Kansas City sprite. I asked him why, and he couldn't offer much in reply. To understand, he said, you had to get to know this Deirdre person, be around her. But I wasn't much interested in being around her; I resented her for turning Joseph's heart away from his own true love.

Their romance didn't last long. Deirdre figured out that Joseph's affections were divided, and she broke it off. By that time, she was already part of my world. During that first summer, Deirdre and I both stayed on campus to work for the school. But I didn't fall in love with her then; I was busy falling in love with someone else. In hindsight, it has the look of providence: because my youthful heart was elsewhere, I was able to see her clearly, to develop a genuine friendship untroubled by the heat in my nineteen-year-old blood and the romantic ideals in my nineteen-year-old mind.

Her reaction to those ideals maddened me. She refused to take me too seriously at a time when I was becoming far too serious, filled with thoughts of nobility and dignity and the rejection of all things base. Deirdre was older, more experienced, and experience had helped to make her balanced where I was extreme. She didn't wilt in the face of my fulminations, but neither did she write me off. She pricked me with barbs of mirthful wit when I needed pricking, and she affirmed what was worthwhile in my efforts by her genuine affection and regard.

Part of that regard was based on my growing attention to the spiritual life. Deirdre had lived on her own for a while and had ceased attending to a faith she never really knew. She came to TAC on the advice of her brother, who also attended, and there discovered Catholicism much more dramatically than I had. Having been away, she was intensely grateful for her return to the church. She was confirmed freshman year and took Maximilian Kolbe, the martyr of Auschwitz, as her confirmation saint. We didn't talk much about the faith, and we didn't take rosary walks, but those times when we did talk about it stayed with her.

In Deirdre, religion was coupled with an already generous spirit, and the consolations of the faith with an easy joy in earthly life. She was fun, infectiously so. Besides working on campus, she waited tables in nearby Ventura. Every night, she returned with libations from Trader Joe's—usually red wine and gin (in those days, the campus ban on alcohol was lifted in summer). The object of my affections at the time was a girl named Sarah, and she and I would hail Deirdre's return as the evening shifted from fledgling courtship to convivial party.

Weekends I spent with Joseph, who was living and working down in Ojai. I think that I was already divining something of the similarity between Deirdre and my friend the poet. It was more than their blond hair and Irish ancestry. Both, I thought, seemed supremely pleased with themselves, forever delighted at the hilarity of their own antics. Both placed high value on comedy as the remedy for everyday ills, but harbored something deeper for deeper troubles. Waugh crystallized it for me in *Brideshead*. After developing a close collegiate friendship with Sebastian Flyte, Charles Ryder finds himself, over a decade later, falling in love with Sebastian's sister Julia. Sebastian, says Charles, "was with me daily in Julia; or rather it was Julia I had known in him, in those distant Arcadian days." Sebastian, he says, "was the forerunner" (ibid., 333).

I broke up with Sarah after Thanksgiving of junior year. By Valentine's Day, I was mad for Deirdre, but I had resolved not to kiss her for at least six months. I did not want her to be a rebound. She kindly followed my lead. We courted our way through second semester without ever speaking of it, now holding hands during *Red Rock West* at Laemmle's Sunset 5 in Los Angeles, now playing footsie under the table during seminar while I argued with my tutor about *The Federalist Papers*. I resisted mightily, and finally broke down late one night just off campus. It wasn't anybody's dream of a first kiss: sitting on the ground near a cattle gate, tired and buzzing, our mouths bone-dry from bourbon.

That kiss was the first of thousands, hours and hours of happy kissing. My understanding of chastity was considerably more nuanced than it had been in high school. I knew now that sexual sin began in the will's surrender to passion, even before any outward act. I knew that sin could be mortal, that it could separate me from the life of God granted to me in baptism. I knew that it was wrong to deliberately place myself in the near occasion of sin. But despite all this new understanding, I still held to my brother's old standard of "never do more than kiss a girl." So we kissed. We kissed in my car, a bottle of wine between us and a candle on the dashboard. We kissed at the beach. And though there was a rule about on-campus displays of affection, we kissed amid the girders of the new library that went up senior year.

Senior year brought fights as we drew closer together and started to rub up against each other's rough edges. (Naturally, I can remember only *her* offenses.) Tom Waits's "Please Call Me, Baby," gained special resonance.

> *The evening fell just like a star*
> *Left a trail behind*
> *You spit as you slammed out the door . . .*

But the year also brought the knowledge that I wanted to marry her. I proposed four months after graduation. She accepted, and we were married the following May. She was barely twenty-five; I was a month shy of my twenty-third birthday. I hadn't planned on marrying young, but there seemed little point in waiting. She was living in Kansas City while I languished in San Diego, and the distance wasn't doing anything except sharpening my desire. Despite frequent visits, the situation was intolerable. I wanted her in my life.

Still, in the months before the wedding, I had several deep moments of doubt. They were more than I knew what to do with, more than I knew how to glean anything from. What was I doing? Was this what I really wanted? Would I run up against Waugh's four-years-in horror? I began to turn inward.

This was contrary to the advice of Father Steckler, who had told me, "A man should think about himself for three minutes a day, during his examination of conscience. After that, he shouldn't be able to stand thinking about himself any more." He was fond of such statements, fond of blowing contrary to the prevailing wind, in this case, the tendency toward intense self-contemplation. I had already discerned that I loved Deirdre and she loved me, seemingly enough to make a lifelong go of it. I had prayed to know God's will in the matter as well, and if prayer had not brought me the peace of certainty, neither did I think it had brought these billowing anxieties.

It was Deirdre who saved me, who showed the truth behind the cliché of "if you love someone, set them free." I finally told her about my fears, a month before the wedding. She replied that she wanted my happiness; if I didn't want to marry her, then I shouldn't do it. If I called it off, she would be sad, but she would survive. In the face of her devotion and strength—qualities in her I was only beginning to fathom—my anxieties burned away.

ᗡᗡᗡᗡᗡ

MY SISTER-IN-LAW LISA attended the John Paul II Institute for Marriage and Family Studies in Washington, D.C. When we get together, there is a lot of talk about the theology of marriage. I enjoy it, and I am grateful that she thinks about these things. Marriage is a sacrament, a visible sign of God's grace. It's good to get expositions of its transcendent quality from somewhere besides the occasional wedding. That transcendent quality, after all, ought to be woven into the mundane, material fabric of matrimony. Myself, I am intellectually lazy. I like to chew things over, but I have neither a ravenous appetite nor a discriminating palate. Like a sea anemone rooted to the ocean floor, I am grounded in my beliefs but am content to feed on whatever the prevailing current sends my way. Unlike the anemone, I know better, and have the power (if not the will) to choose better waters than I do.

One morsel that stuck in my craw: the question of marriage's primary end. Before getting married, I lived with another TAC graduate for a few months. From him, I learned that the 1917 *Code of Canon Law* had stated that the primary end of marriage was the procreation and education of offspring. The secondary ends, those of "mutual help" and the "remedy for concupiscence" were subordinate to the former. In 1944, the Holy See had affirmed this teaching, against the notion that the subordinate ends were on an equal footing with the primary end.

This news came as a bit of a shock. I wanted to get married to join my life to Deirdre's. I knew that the marriage ceremony included a promise to God that I would accept children, and I was ready to accept children—eventually, anyway. But making babies was not why I proposed. If what the church proposed was true, it was a truth that ran counter to my experience. That was new. The existence of God, fallen nature, even the admonition against contraception—all these made sense to me. They fit into my perception of the scheme of things. Other doctrines may not have been as manifest, but neither were they contrary to my sense of the world.

Gaudiem et Spes, the Pastoral Constitution on the Church in the Modern World that came out of Vatican II, toned down the distinction, saying, "By its very nature the institution of marriage and married love is ordered to the procreation and education of the offspring and it is in them that it finds its crowning glory. Children are the supreme gift of marriage and contribute greatly to the good of the parents themselves" (Austin Flannery, O.P., ed., *"Gaudiem et Spes"* in *Vatican Council II: The Conciliar and Post Conciliar Documents* [Northport, NY: Costello Publishing Company, 1987], 950, 953). "Supreme gift" and "crowning glory" do not necessarily mean "primary end," but they can be read as supporting that notion.

But the *Catechism*, while it quotes *Gaudiem et Spes* on this subject, opens its discussion of marriage by referencing the 1983 *Code of Canon Law* (available on www.vatican.va), which states that marriage "is ordered to the well-being of the spouses and to the procreation and upbringing of children." The secondary end of "mutual help," here expressed as "the well-being of the spouses," had been raised up to the point of being mentioned first.

I DO NOT PRETEND TO KNOW the workings of the church, the events or reasons behind such a change. Nor am I a learned theologian, someone schooled enough in the church's thinking to offer a plausible account. But as someone who has sought to conform to both ends of the sacrament, I would like to offer my own account of "the well-being of the spouses."

I think my relationship with my wife is the best chance I will ever have to love my neighbor as myself. My success or failure as a lover will show most clearly with her. She is my best occasion for self-sacrifice, the bloodless martyrdom of daily life. My children also demand self-sacrifice, and on a greater scale, but there is a mandatory element to my fatherly efforts. They are my children; their dependence on me is nearly total. To neglect them would be an obvious moral failure. Even when they are at their worst, I do not wish they would raise themselves. Deirdre is another story. She is far more autonomous; she took care of herself before we married. I sometimes wish that she would do for herself some of the things she asks of me. I like to sit and read and be left alone. Overcoming that wish to the point of granting her requests cheerfully, or even anticipating them, is a small but constant opportunity for charity.

She is my best lesson in the pain of sin. The relative innocence of children may make them ideal candidates as earthly stand-ins for God. When you sin against them, the injustice of it shines forth—they're just kids. But Deirdre loves me as no other, and I her. When I sin against her—when I break a promise, speak a cutting word, or fail in my duty—I see the pain in her face, and the ingratitude of it hits home. How can I wound one who loves me so well? I see the wild incongruity of it: I love her so much in my better moments, the good she does is the source of so much of my happiness; how can I forget this? My kids make me happy, but there is less goodwill on their part, less effort, less sacrifice.

There is perhaps an element of self-interested imperfection in loving Deirdre, since I may justly ask for some return. She is, after all, my greatest earthly joy. Better, maybe, to have daily encounters with a truly difficult person—to love a wretch would be more impressive. Better, maybe, to learn love through children, who are still learning to be grateful, and to love when love is difficult. But in some way, also easier. No one can wound me like my wife. Her failures, even in matters as simple as listening and understanding, cut deeper than anyone else's failure, because we are one.

There are many different sorts of marriages, and I do not stand in judgment over them. Nor do I sit in judgment on the church's earlier teaching. But in my experience of marriage, the unitive end rightfully stands beside the procreative. The joy of heaven comes from union with God, the supreme union of lover and beloved. Until that union—pray God—comes to pass, I have a foretaste of that joy in marriage, an echo of heaven on earth.

_ഔ ഔ ഔ ഔ ഔ_

do you need to be a paterfamilias?

THE LIBERAL ARTS ARE USELESS. They are called liberal because they are not servile. One does not study them for the sake of something else, as one might study law to become a lawyer. One studies them for their own sake. Philosophy perfects man as a knowing animal, not man as an engineer. That was our mantra at TAC, one I happily accepted. But come senior year, the practical reasserts itself. What are you going to do upon graduation—especially you there, who is thinking about marriage?

My first thought was more school, more school and a great ball of debt chained to my ankle. Debt from school, debt from living expenses during school. Though my mother and father had gotten their master's degrees before marrying, my father had still been facing his doctoral work. My brother Mark and sister-in-law Lisa were in grad school when they tied the knot, pursuing degrees in theology. More school seemed like the thing to do.

Deirdre, who hoped I would propose but wasn't going to sit around waiting, decided to enroll in a Physical Therapist's

Assistant program back in Kansas City. Her mom was a nurse, so it was a little like entering the family business. So what about me? Clinical psychology was the answer that came creeping miserably into my mind. From future priest to future psychologist; how I squirmed when reading Walker Percy's *Lancelot*, in which the patient-penitent castigates the psychologist-priest for not knowing which one he is or what he is about. Still, I liked the idea of clinical psych well enough; people interested me, and I had something of an unconscious knack for getting them to talk. But egad! Two years of undergraduate studies just to pick up enough psychology to take the Psych GRE. After that, grad school. Ugh.

৯৫৯৫৯৫৯৫

"*I DON'T KNOW* what I'm going to do for a job after college, Pap."

"Well, go see your ward leader."

Pappy was my maternal grandfather. When he said that, just before my senior year, he was a few months from his grave. I don't know if he was joking, or if he really thought nineties Cortland boasted a political machine in the manner of pre-seventies Albany, or if his mind was just slipping a gear, dropping into another time and place. I do know that his own career had landed in his lap, that a stint with the county morgue had ended suddenly with a phone call that eventually led to a position representing New York City's interests to the state legislature. So after he died in October, I started praying to him that the same sort of thing would happen to me. I had never prayed to deceased relatives before (and cannot recall praying to the saints prior to attending college). But now, I was moved to do so.

Three months later, I was standing outside my thesis advisor's office, waiting for a meeting. The college's career advisor, a tutor whose office happened to be next door, suddenly came out and asked, "You want to be a journalist, right?" I suppose he had gotten this idea from the zine I was putting out yearly and selling around campus, usually to pay off speeding tickets. I called it *The Hype*, a short form of its original title, *The Hyperborean*—named after a mythological, unfallen race.

The zine was an uneven thing; it was murder getting people to write and submit anything, even poetry. But we did have fun. A tutor submitted a poem containing a verse in Greek, complete with translation and phonetic footnotes. I did my best Joseph Mitchell impersonation, writing about a visit Deirdre and I paid to a dive bar in Ventura. And my roommate Jon and I wrote poems in praise of The Pit. His unvarnished paean ended with the splendid, spare refrain, *I go down to the pit / I drink a lot / I go down to the pit / It's a parking lot.*

"Sure," I answered the advisor, having never given the possibility of journalism much thought. He told me that the weekly newspaper the *San Diego Reader* was looking to hire a graduate. I called the editor, Jim Holman, met him for an interview, and started at the *Reader* on a trial basis in May of 1995. Ten years later, I am still there. I give the credit to my grandfather; I believe he heard my prayers.

This is the story I tell when people ask me how I got into journalism. When I tell it, I am conscious that my listener will probably think I am a loon. Usually, that kind of consciousness leaves me stammering with embarrassment at what I am proposing. But when I tell this story, I do not stammer. I do not much care if my listener thinks I am a loon. Maybe it's because I love Pappy enough that I want to give him the credit, regardless of the effect.

SO I BECAME, in Joseph's words, a scribbler, and a happy one at that. When a neighbor asked me in 2001 if I dreamed of writing fiction, my "no" was an honest one. But it didn't last. Scenes began to coalesce in my imagination. I started jotting down descriptive paragraphs. A little while later, I got a call from my editor. She is an accomplished writer, and I admire her work. She has been something of a mentor to me, and I give her words considerable weight, which explains the impact of the following.

"Can I ask you a personal question?"

"Yes."

"Do you need to be a paterfamilias? Or could you be satisfied with two or three children? You could be a real writer if you gave yourself to it and really worked at it. I think it's something that you have to consider."

A hard question, and it hit home even as I registered my silent protests. It is true that I feel a sort of primitive pleasure in the notion of gathering my many children about me. Of the blessings promised to God's faithful, one of my favorites is this: "Your wife shall be like a fruitful vine in the recesses of your home, your children like olive plants around your table." I feel unfettered delight every time I hear it read, happy to interpret it literally as the barren age withers about me. I am in what a more weathered parent might call the sweet, early stages of parenting. My four children—Finian, seven; Isaac, five; Olivia, three; and Elijah, eighteen months—are a great drain on my energies. They are also a great delight. I have not entered the war years of adolescence.

But I never explicitly wanted to be a paterfamilias, never thought of being satisfied or unsatisfied with *x* number of kids. I imagine I could be satisfied with four. (When I had two, I imagined I could be satisfied with two. But after a while,

Deirdre and I felt a gap, a space that wanted filling. That was one of the closest things to a spiritual prompting I've ever experienced.) Being a paterfamilias would be hard. It would mean providing for all those olive plants around my table. Even now, that thought routinely grips my gut with iron tongs of fear. And then there are the matters of giving my children a decent upbringing, providing an introduction to the world, passing on the faith, etc.

THE CATHOLIC CHURCH TEACHES that contraceptive acts are "intrinsically evil." However, it also teaches that it is morally licit to abstain from sex for the sake of avoiding pregnancy when there are "grave reasons" for doing so. If you assent to these teachings, the question then becomes, what constitutes "grave reasons"? Whatever talent for writing I possess is a gift from God. Is a desire (also God-given?) to write for art's sake a grave enough reason for avoiding more children? I see my mentor's point—being a paterfamilias, the lord of a large household, seems incompatible with spending the requisite hours to write and rewrite. Either the children or the work would suffer. It seemed so even from the vantage point of two kids.

On the heels of this comes the question of God's will for a given man. My friend Ernie sees his job, first and foremost, as an instrument through which he may provide for his family. Being a husband and father is his real work, and to a significant degree, it is mine as well. I suspect that he believes children in quantity to be part of the deal when you get married. *Gaudiem et Spes*, while affirming that couples must use judgment in these matters, took time to make "special mention" of those "who after prudent reflection and common decision generously undertake the proper upbringing of a large number of children" (Austin Flannery, O.P., ed., *"Gaudiem et Spes"* in *Vatican Council II: The Conciliar and Post Conciliar Documents* [Northport, NY: Costello Publishing Company, 1987], 954). You don't limit kids because you think you might have another calling, Ernie might say. Weigh a doubt ("God wants you to write") against a certainty ("You are married") and carry on.

My brother, Mark, took a different approach. When he found himself out of a job in the summer of 1996, he started considering a parish position in Louisiana. He didn't want to move so far from family, and he didn't really want the job, but he was prepared to grit his teeth and provide for his wife and children. But Mom encouraged him to do what he thought God was calling him to do, and he decided to enroll in film school. After that, he and his family lived with Mom and Dad for two and a half years while he looked for work in the field. For a time, he was willing to put his calling ahead of bringing home the bacon.

I DIDN'T HAVE A CLEAR ANSWER to my mentor's question. I muddled along, fitfully banging out great chunks of prose until I had the rough draft of the middle third of a novel. Then I stopped. I had let my newspaper writing slide for too long, and was bringing financial woe to my wife. I sent the section to my agent, who had taken me on after reading an earlier manuscript, a memoir about being a new father. Sending the middle third was a sorry thing to do, but my faith was weak. I wanted affirmation from an earthly source. I wanted my agent to tell me I wasn't wasting my time—my time and my family's time. I began to wait, and I began to pray.

On the happy side, it wasn't the sort of prayer that inspires pride. I didn't have to fight the Christian sin of congratulating myself for my advancing holiness: "I've risen from the muck!" as opposed to "I've been raised up!" As if rising were not, like everything else, the result of grace. If anything, the prayer heightened my sense of utter dependence on God. There was nothing else I could do.

Though my prayer included a petition—a daily request that St. Thérèse of Lisieux intercede on my behalf—the bulk of it was a condensed form of the Liturgy of the Hours, which I found in a monthly publication called *Magnificat*. Daily, I read a hymn, a psalm, a passage from Scripture, the Canticle of Zechariah, a list of intercessions, the Our Father, the Mass readings, and a meditation. But however manifold the form, however much I praised and repented and contemplated, I couldn't shake the feeling that it was all one grand request. "Do this, please. I'm not really seeking first the kingdom of God, but couldn't you add this one thing unto me just to get me started?" Like a child, I sometimes viewed the mere fact that I was praying as a spiritual bargaining chip: "Look, I'm giving you the beginning of my day. I'm offering you these prayers. Can't you do this for me in return?"

A MONTH BECAME SIX WEEKS. I received an e-mail from my brother, who may have guessed at my anxiety through his own frustrations. What he wrote sounded like a gloss on what my mother gets at when she tells me, "Whatever God wants."

"The more I pray about this," wrote Mark, "the more I get the sense that it is absolute folly to measure ourselves as artists by what somebody else knows or doesn't know, thinks or doesn't think, about us. The *only thing* that matters is: are we inspired? And if we are, if what we do is from God, who is the very source of all beauty, what more does the artist need to know than that? We could write a book or a poem or a song, or even write or make a film that almost no one knows about, either before or after we're dead. But if God sees and declares what we have made to be beautiful, Who knows better than He whether we have been 'successful'?"

I lacked Mark's conviction. I feared that if I adopted this outlook, it would be merely the self-soothing of the unappreciated Christian artist. But then I recalled a line from the movie *Babette's Feast*. The fading opera star Achille Papin has visited a tiny village and discovered a woman who will become the toast of Europe, so wondrous is her voice. The woman's father allows Papin to train her, but will not allow her to leave. He is a minister; he will have his daughter's voice used solely for the praise of God. Papin departs, heartbroken. But he does not forget, and years later, he writes her a letter in which he takes comfort from a sublime expectation: "How your singing will delight the angels!"

I thought of Richard Yates. When Blake Bailey's biography of Yates came out in 2003, the thing I kept reading in the reviews was how few people read this brilliant writer Yates, how unappreciated he was. What if only one hundred people had ever read *Revolutionary Road*? Wouldn't it still be a great novel? What about fifty people? Twenty-five? Ten? The artist craves an audience and is trying to communicate something to that audience. But the failure to find one is not the same as failing to make good art.

I got an answer to my prayer before I got an answer from my agent. It came during Mass, one of those rare moments when a thought springs up and feels just awkward enough to have hailed not from my own musings, but from the Lord. "You must slay your ambition." I hadn't thought I was ambitious. I had thought I was insecure and in need of encouragement. Apparently, God knew better. I tried to give it up, tried not to let the silence from New York tinge each day with disappointment. Weeks later, my agent got back to me. She said she wasn't wild about the novel, but that she would read it when it was finished.

⁖⁖⁖⁖⁖

sex and the outrageous principle

I WAS A VIRGIN WHEN I MARRIED, an achievement best credited to grace, formation, and the avoidance of the occasion. I remained a virgin for the first four days of my marriage, an achievement best credited to a strong desire not to conceive a child. To a young Catholic trying to toe the party line, it can seem a cruel joke—you manage to save sex for the marriage bed, only to arrive and find the event cancelled due to ovulation. Deirdre and I spent our wedding night at the Ritz Carlton overlooking the Plaza in Kansas City; my new father-in-law jokingly threatened to gather a band to perform outside our window. Would I have requested a dirge or a lullaby?

I abstained because I accept the teaching of the church when it states in the *Catechism* that "'every action which, whether in anticipation of the conjugal act, or in its accomplishment, or in the development of its natural consequences, proposes, whether as an end or as a means, to render procreation impossible' is intrinsically evil" (*Catechism of the Catholic Church* [Boston: Pauline Books & Media, 1994], 570). In other words, contraception before, during, or after sex is forbidden. In fact, "each and every marriage act must remain open to the transmission of life" (ibid., 569). Inherent in each marital act is "a connection, established by God, which man on his own initiative may not break, between the unitive significance and the procreative significance." That "each and every" eliminates the standard sexual substitutes of masturbation and oral sex.

If you don't want to conceive, you're left with Natural Family Planning—monitoring the woman's temperature and cervical mucous for signs of fertility and abstaining from sex accordingly. (NFP works—my brother and his wife, who were both attending graduate school when they married, waited two and a half years to conceive their first child.)

The church proposes that this teaching can be arrived at through reason. It's not simply an article of faith, like the Immaculate Conception. And once or twice, during conversations with Mark and Lisa, I think I have understood that argument for a moment, as if seeing a landscape illuminated by lightning. But the brilliant burst fades, and I am left with only indistinct memory.

So why do I accept the teaching? Because it has been the consistent teaching of the church for centuries. It has the weight of tradition behind it, the same tradition that has handed down to me so many things that I accept without protest. Three persons in one God; two natures in the one person of Christ. If I understood these ideas when we discussed them in senior theology, it was another lightning-flash moment. Happily, I do not regard understanding on my part to be essential to that acceptance.

I have other reasons. One of them has to do with the integrity of the faith, the "all-or-nothing" that Father Paneloux proposed in *The Plague*. If I say the faith is true except for *this one thing*, then is not the entire edifice weakened? In both the Apostle's Creed and the Nicene Creed, I profess to believe in the Catholic Church. If I deny her consistent teaching, can I really make that profession of faith? And on what authority do I make my judgment? If I believe that Christ founded the church, and that it operates under the guidance of the Holy Spirit, what does it mean for me to reject this or that teaching?

Finally, I have the saints. Over and over, again and again, the saints point to humility and obedience as the surest paths for advancing in holiness. It requires humility to accept a teaching I do not fully understand. Obedience to the teaching about married sexuality is difficult. Even if the teaching was incorrect, I believe God would be pleased by my submission—"not my will, but thine" (Luke 22:42). Still, that was cold comfort during those first four nights. The Bible compares a bridegroom's rejoicing over his bride to Christ's rejoicing over his church. I had long been fond of the advice from Proverbs about the wife of one's youth: "Let her breasts inebriate thee always" (Proverbs 5:19). The ecstasy of sex serves as an analogue of the joy of heavenly union. And here was I, holding off.

I held off because I wanted a year to rejoice over my bride before we conceived, to develop the ease of living together, and to solidify the marital bonds between us. That was grave enough reason for us; we felt we were building the foundation for the family to come.

I DID OKAY FOR THREE MONTHS. By "okay," I mean I merely pestered my poor bride incessantly for sex during our periods of abstention, without quite breaking down and saying, "Bring on the kids; I want lovin'!" I worked at home in our one-bedroom apartment. I was constantly aware of her presence. This beautiful woman; this beautiful, available woman. I had waited so long, and now here she was, all the time, in love with me and I with her, our union blessed and approved by God. Oh, God.

I wanted *it*, but I didn't want *them*, and Deirdre was forced again and again to confront me with this fact. My halfhearted demands made her feel like I was accusing her of holding out, like it was somehow her fault for being fertile. Hardly loving; hardly the spirit of Natural Family Planning. But I didn't reform. I made up songs.

To the tune of "The Twelve Days of Christmas":

> *On the fifth day of Dry Times my true love said to me,*
> *At least a week*
> *The chart says I'm fertile*
> *My fluid's stretchy*
> *Let's hold hands*
> *And you can't have any more nookie.*

It got to the point where I scratched "nookie" in the leather of my shoe with my fingernail, pleading with every step I took around our home. Deirdre has never forgotten this. During that third month, we got lazy about charting the signs, and a slight milkiness in her mucous was all the sign I needed that we were good to go. Needless to say, we conceived.

Deirdre got a yeast infection, then missed her period. We went to a women's health clinic. The nurse chuckled as she told my wife she was pregnant—of course! My wife came out and told me the news with an air of quiet excitement. I was, ridiculously, stunned. While she paid the bill, I left the clinic's lobby and stepped out onto a concrete balcony. I actually stared at the sky.

I knew that I would eventually become a father. I did not want to become a father yet. I was twenty-three; I was terrified. I offered God an absurd deal (there I go again, bargaining with God): if I surrendered my will and accepted this child, perhaps he would then take it away. Perhaps my wife would miscarry. Perhaps this could all be just a test. I held on to that notion for maybe three days before I finally surrendered and accepted that my wife was pregnant and was likely to stay that way until the birth of our first child.

Opponents of abortion are fond of this quote from Mother Teresa: "It is a poverty that a child must die so that you may live as you wish." Procuring an abortion never entered my mind. Instead, I asked for one from God. I asked Him to terminate the pregnancy. God, of course, would not be culpable; as the author of life, He may take life when He wishes. And I would have had no active part in the abortion, except that I would have prayed for it. My firstborn son is seven now, and seeing him in all his manifest personhood makes my reaction seem monstrous. I see the truth in Mother Teresa's claim: what a tremendous poverty to have wished that he go away and leave me in peace.

ᴓᴓᴓᴓᴓ

MINE WAS A POVERTY OF SOUL. What about physical poverty? What about the billions of people who don't happen to be comfortably employed denizens of Southern California? Fair enough. On October 9 of 2002, the Web site for the satirical newspaper *The Onion* ran a feature titled, "Starving Third World Masses Warned against Evils of Contraception" (*The Onion*, 9 October 2002).

In the article, a missionary in Calcutta, "a city where 53 percent of residents are under 18," tells villagers, "God does not want you to choke the rivers of fertile bounty with immoral birth-control pills. He wants you to continue expanding your families. If your babies starve, Jesus will forgive them." A resident of Bogotá assents, saying, "Life in this shantytown is difficult, but our troubles are nothing compared to what we will face in the Lake of Fire if we try to live within our means and regulate the number of offspring we produce, as Satan teaches." Natural Family Planning—here equated with the "rhythm method"—comes in for a parting shot, naturally. It is cited as being 87 percent effective (I think it's closer to 98 percent), which, according to a cardinal, "is more than suitable for maintaining a reasonable household. So long as no seed is spilled, God will not immediately strike you down."

I love *The Onion*. I love the way it skewers the accepted absurd. I weep with laughter over stories like "Ant Farm Teaches Children About Toil, Death." And I sometimes chuckle over their take on the church: "Pope Calls for Greater Understanding Between Catholics, Hellbound." I didn't chuckle over the contraception article, and there was a time when it would have left me spluttering with fury—the distortions! The oversimplification! The misinterpretation!

But that was before Planned Parenthood began the side-of-the-bus ad campaign that featured an African mother and her undernourished baby. The caption read something like, "As long as there is a Third World, we can never be One World." The message was clear: as long as overpopulated, impoverished people are denied access to birth control, they will remain overpopulated and impoverished. And that is intolerable.

Deirdre was upset by the ad. I agreed that it felt disingenuous—I'm not ready to grant the pure, uninterested goodwill that Planned Parenthood claims as a motive. But I wasn't outraged. I found myself thinking of the outrage that a Planned

Parenthood supporter might feel if I were to tell them what I believed. Namely: for a child to be born into a life of unremitted misery is a terrible thing, but for a man and woman to take part in a contraceptive act to prevent such a birth is worse.

THE STATEMENT IS OUTRAGEOUS, and it is backed by an equally outrageous principle: death before sin, even the death of another, even the death of a child. Though I suppose it is possible to sin against prudence—and even against charity—in deciding to conceive a child, it is still only *possible*. Conception is never *intrinsically* evil, but contraception always is so.

The non-Christian world is not unfamiliar with the idea of dying for a principle, and it probably bears the Christian martyrs some measure of respect for their integrity and commitment. But here, the Planned Parenthood supporter would be listening to me uphold an ideal that might mean the suffering and death of thousands (millions?) of people other than myself. I imagine this is what gets some people upset about the pope's statements on human sexuality: "The man isn't even married; what can he possibly have to tell me? How can he be so arrogant as to make such claims?" Likewise, how can *I* be so arrogant as to make such claims?

I can make them because I believe in that preposterous-sounding Lake of Fire, or at least its spiritual equivalent. I believe in hell—eternal separation from God—though I do not presume to judge who will be sent there. I also believe in heaven, where Lazarus was taken after spending a wretched life starving at the rich man's gate. I can make those claims because I believe that suffering is not the greatest evil in this world. "Do not fear those who can harm the body; rather, fear the one who can kill the soul." The martyrs would not deny their faith in the face of suffering; how can I?

The Christian walks in the world, and may share many virtues with his non-Christian fellows. But eventually, and at crucial junctures, they will part company.

꩜꩜꩜꩜꩜

why so many?

"WHY SO MANY?"

That was the question asked of my friend Mary when she was expecting her fourth child. Her interrogator was a complete stranger. The rejection of contraception, tied up as it is with the intimacy of the marriage bed, might be something a person would like to keep relatively private. But the signs of Mary's bedroom habits were all around her—in her belly, in her arms, tugging at her shirt. . . . And because her sex life had been made public in this way, the stranger was emboldened to inquire. At least it was better than what Mary's husband, Ernie, got from a loan officer when he applied to borrow money for a van: "What are you, rabbits?"

Other gems:

"You know how those are made, don't you?"

"Time for separate beds!"

"What are you going to do about this?"

"That's enough, now."

"Damn, son, you've screwed yourself out of a place at the table!" (Actually, that one is kind of funny.)

"WHY SO MANY?"

Part of the problem with this last one is that the question was deathly serious, but the stranger asking it wasn't. She wasn't after an account of faith and its effect on Mary's life. She was amazed and curious, her reaction akin to that of a spectator at a circus sideshow.

Mary is wounded by this treatment, worn down by the dirty looks she gets when she goes out with all her children, worried that if any one of them is poorly behaved, or shoeless, or begging for attention, she will incur judgment from those around her. She does not worry about people thinking ill of her. She worries that, unless she is always in peak form, unless her children always make a fine appearance, people will wag their heads over "people with large families." *Tsk, tsk. Poor woman. How she must suffer.*

She does suffer. So does my sister-in-law Lisa, who runs into the same sort of thing. But it's not all suffering. Lisa once wrote a story for the diocesan paper of LaCrosse, Wisconsin about being a mother of five (Lisa Lickona, "Crazy but Good," *The Catholic Times*, 16 August 2001, 21). She wrote that people who judged her situation from outside could "never glimpse the quiet moments of joy and peace—what happens in the depths of my heart." She told a story of struggling to get all the kids out the door for a walk, three weeks after her fourth and fifth children (twins!) were born.

"Yes, this is crazy," she concluded. "And it is real, and it is beautiful. Max ran down the sidewalk, full of boyish delight, stopping only to point in awe at each passing car. Monica and Kate chatted. The babies blinked in the sun. I had, of course, forgotten their bonnets. So we made a little game of running through the sunny patches of sidewalk, chanting, 'Quick, quick, quick.' And then we all dragged our heels in the shade. 'Slow, slow, slow.' 'It's like learning to dance,' I mused to myself, remembering the fox-trot, 'Slow, slow, quick, quick.' I knew I was happy. Children can do this to you, especially in numbers. It is a joyful, buoyant kind of happiness that you can get from nothing else in life. Yes, this is crazy. And it is good."

Still, the question rankles me: "Why so many?" It makes me long to fire back with sarcasm. "Because I'm a mindless automaton Catholic in the thrall of a castrated hierarchy that supposes sex to be evil if it doesn't lead directly to procreation and seeks to oppress women by saddling them with hordes of mewling brats."

Or: "Why so few?"

Or, with perfect piety: "Because a life pleasing to God consists in self-sacrifice, and accepting many children necessitates such self-sacrifice."

Or, in a bitter attempt at humor: "Because Saint Catherine of Siena was born the last of twenty-five children. We want to improve our chances of spawning a doctor of the church."

Or, with pointed politeness: "That's a rather personal question, don't you think?"

But I will not fire back. The sight of four children makes most people assume I'm a Catholic, or maybe a Mormon. This immediately puts me at a disadvantage. I do not like to lead with my Catholicism. I prefer, if I can, to first win people's affection and regard. When it comes out that I am one of those awful Catholics, there will be something to weigh in the balance. But if they know my faith going in, if they see in my kids a testament of my opposition to contraception, their hackles may be raised. This is not the time for confrontation, even if it's invited. And so, I will usually say something inoffensive yet honest, something like, "Because every time we ask our kids if they want another brother or sister, they say yes." It's probably not the best thing to say, because it's not the real determining factor. But it's true, and it sounds sweet, and it's what happened to come out of my mouth one time.

I can sympathize with my interrogator. A lion in one of Aesop's fables is asked by the other beasts—themselves the proud parents of large broods—how many children he has. The lion replies, "Only one. But that one is a *lion*." The moral is that it's quality, not quantity that counts. How easy it is to simply substitute humans for beasts and let the story stand. And the quality of the children aside, haven't we learned that man should aspire to wisdom and culture—rather than simple multiplication—as a means of achieving greatness? Again, I see the point. More kids mean less time for me.

WHEN DEIRDRE AND I WERE FIRST MARRIED, I made a new dessert for every gathering—croissant-bread pudding with Riesling-poached pears, triple-berry shortcake with white chocolate mousse, vanilla-hazelnut cheesecake. Friends came and stayed for days; we rose late and hung out in the kitchen all afternoon, nipping at bread and cheese and sipping wine while Deirdre made dinner and I wrestled with my latest confection. Then we feasted and drank late into the night. We subscribed to *Cook's Illustrated* and *Saveur*; we worked from the recipes of Julia Child and marveled at the creations in *The French Laundry Cookbook*. I loved being a foodie. The pleasures it brought felt honest and substantial. And my desserts made Deirdre happy.

Those days have not disappeared completely. We still have friends visit, still drink plenty of wine, still gather over well-laid tables. But I haven't made a new dessert in years, and often, I don't make one at all. Baking, for me, takes time and concentration, and periods of prolonged tranquility tend to be in short supply when company comes. The quiet morning hours in an empty kitchen after breakfast are no more.

This bothers me some, but it doesn't really hurt. I have become a sort of conscious peasant, forcing myself into a simpler life by increasing my household. If that means grilling a marinated tri-tip of beef and whipping out a basic chocolate cake instead of lobster crepes and pear *tarte tatin*, so be it. If in years to come it means burgers and apple crisp, so be that as well.

It's not simply a matter of choosing fecundity over the good life, finding fulfillment in kids instead of cash or culture. Though children are fulfilling—a frequent reminder of the old saw that the best way to be happy is to concentrate on someone else's happiness—they are not a means to an end. They are an end in themselves. That's another reason why I won't answer the question, "Why so many?" It's hard to explain that I'm not doing it for me, not primarily, anyway. That's why I wince when I hear someone say, "I want to have *x* number of children." When the "I" is doing such definitive planning, I fear a note of self-absorption where none is permissible, fear a view of children as simply an extension of the self, rather like the old idea of gaining immortality through descendants. Is there in such a statement an interest in the child for the child's sake or in the child for the parent's sake?

That's not to say that planning is wrong. When Deirdre and I took a class in Natural Family Planning, our instructor told us that couples should come together every month and prayerfully consider whether God was calling them to try to conceive. The idea was not simply to crank 'em out and make more souls for heaven, but to cooperate with God's will for your life and the life of your family. I don't pretend to know how many kids God wants any other couple to have; Deirdre and I both had happy childhoods with just one sibling. I don't even know how many kids God wants *us* to have, though it seems we're headed for more.

෨෨෨෨෨

MY FAITH IS WEAK; I am anxious when I think about the future. I have trouble considering the lilies of the field. I ought to trust in the Lord, I know; it's His will I'm trying to obey. But He has been known to give crosses as gifts, so I often look elsewhere for comfort. I imagine other, secondary goods, other benefits to this large family of mine.

One of those goods is the creation of my own little culture, a community whose primacy is sufficient to withstand the buffets of a world that regards the faith as folly, or worse. By this, I do not mean an isolated compound in the hinterlands, though the idea is not without appeal, especially as regards the raising of children. Children are sponges, and they are not overly careful about what they absorb. I am in no hurry for them to soak up the sugary sludge being aimed at kids: the worship of cool, of stuff, of empty distraction. Nor am I eager for them to join the ranks of the prematurely sexualized. I think multiple kids can be a help. More kids means less stuff per kid and more sharing. More kids means learning to live (and work) in a community of peers, to forgive others' shortcomings, and to work on correcting your own. More kids runs counter to the cult of cool—who can be cool when changing a diaper?

More important matters: when my children were baptized, Deirdre and I were named their first teachers in the faith. St. Augustine called the home the domestic church. Their formation as Christians is my responsibility. I do not want my children to be insular, incapable of dealing with people different from themselves. I do not want them to believe that we are to huddle in the church's bosom, that we are not required to bear God's love to the world. But now, they are children; they are not yet equipped to be missionaries. Before they go out into the unbelieving world, I want them to sense the worth of what I have taught them.

Kids talk to each other about God. I hear my two eldest boys working out their own questions about God's activity, hammering out the implications of his omnipresence and omniscience. Already, they share a faith. When I was Fin's age, my next-door neighbor told me the Gospels were just made up by four guys a long time ago. You could tell because the stories didn't match up. I believed my parents when they told me the kid was wrong. But if I hadn't—if I had decided that my parents were mistaken—I still would have had my brother's faith to consider. If someone makes an argument like that to Fin, he has more than just his parents' word to rely on. He has a community. It's a bigger base from which to branch out, a bigger support to fall back on.

Even without outside interference, there may come a day when anything I say sounds to Fin like purest idiocy—adolescence is not always kind to fathers. But if that day comes, I hope that rejecting Dad won't mean rejecting the faith, because the faith won't just be mine, or Deirdre's. It'll be the faith of the community.

ᔪᕆᔪᕆᔪᕆ

the roach and the woman

MY FIRST APARTMENT IN SAN DIEGO occupied the bottom-right quarter of a four-unit, pink-and-white stucco house situated next to a Thai restaurant on Fifth Avenue. I found it by skirting the city's magnificent Balboa Park, looking for For Rent signs and assessing the neighborhood from my car. I liked the look of the Hillcrest area—lots of little shops and restaurants—and when I got inside the apartment, I fell in love. Cove ceilings, wood floors, sash-weighted windows just like the ones back east. And the walls were painted the palest imaginable shade of pink, as if they were white, but forever illumined by the last glimmer of sunset. It had only one bedroom, and I was going to have a roommate, but I offered to pay more rent, and he agreed to sleep on a futon in the dining room.

Soon after finding the place, I took a proper look around the neighborhood, on foot. I was delighted to find David's, a good coffee shop with great scones just a few doors down. Another block, and I hit upon an old one-screen movie theater, three used bookstores, and a Jamba Juice. In between, at the corner of Fifth and Robinson, I found a bar, The Brass Rail. A banner hung against the exterior wall: Whipped-Cream Wrestling with the Go-Go Boys, Wednesdays, 9:00 p.m. Together with my older, muscular roommate (another TAC grad), I had just moved into a one-bedroom apartment in the heart of the gay district. What must the neighbors think?

My roommate, heading out one evening: "I'm going down to the chapel at Mercy hospital."

Me, in mock reproach: "You know, it's really sad the way you lie about being pious in order to hide the fact that you're the odds-on favorite in tonight's whipped-cream Wrestlemania."

"I know, I know."

"Go get 'em, tiger!"

And off he went to pray while I read, nursed my cognac, and pined for my beloved Deirdre as she tended bar in Kansas City. Eight months later, I drove east into the heartland, married her, and brought her back to my lovely pink apartment. My roommate moved out. *Now* what must the neighbors think?

ᴏᴏᴏᴏᴏ

WE LIKED HILLCREST. It was a walkable neighborhood. Extraordinary Desserts, easily the best in town, was just down the street. Deirdre got a job waitressing at a tapas restaurant just a few blocks away. I browsed purposefully in the used bookstores, and found a home-furnishings emporium that boasted the finest collection of Russian icons I had ever seen outside a museum. But we left the neighborhood a few months later, when I happened upon a newly vacant two-bedroom guesthouse in nearby South Mission Hills. *That* was a proper love nest, a secluded two-story Spanish bungalow built against a hill, with a fireplace and an isinglass chandelier in the big bedroom. Our neighbors told us it had been used as a brothel during World War II. The main house, at the top of the hill, featured a master suite with walls of bloodiest red, textured to appear as melted wax. We believed our neighbors.

Then we found out Deirdre was pregnant. We started thinking about the curving concrete stairs leading up to the house, the stairs inside that had no banister, the great window right next to our bed that we flung open every morning. We started thinking about moving. And when Deirdre came back from a visit to Kansas City full of a friend's thoughts about the glories of home ownership, I got the bug. Three months later, we settled into a two-bedroom Craftsman in Normal Heights. One story, a patio and a little triangular patch of yard, no dining room, but a spacious kitchen—a great first house. Except for the cockroaches.

A six-foot concrete wall separated our house from the alley behind it. While it provided privacy, it did nothing to keep out the Led Zeppelin booming from the apartments across the way, and it did nothing to keep out the roaches. Roaches were new for me; as far as I knew, we didn't have them in upstate New York. I made it through the first nineteen years of my life without ever seeing a roach in the hard-shelled flesh. On a visit to my brother's, then attending Catholic University in the damp environs of Washington, D.C., I got a taste of what was to come. I discovered what vermin can do to a man; in particular, what a roach can do to a man in love; in particular, what a roach can do to a man in love with a woman who comes unhinged at the sight of a cockroach.

Lisa wasn't home at the time, so I didn't get to see her unhinging. But I could guess at its intensity by observing the intensity of Mark's reaction. He spotted the roach in the apartment's bedroom, growled an expletive, grabbed a shoe, and dove at it. He missed. My stomach gave a little jump at its quickness, the speed with which it stopped and changed directions in the course of its flight, like a fly does in midair. I imagined hearing the superquick tappings of its little feet as it scuttled under the bed. Like a cat that has missed its pounce, Mark was down on his belly, talking in a low tone of controlled rage: "Where are you, you son of a bitch?"

Such behavior is strange for my family. My father had always stressed the importance of closing screen doors so that flies didn't get into the house. When we forgot and let a fly slip inside, Dad spent however long it took to capture the pest. With religious patience, he stalked it, slowly lowering a glass over its resting spot on a wall, only to have it dash sideways and away. Over and over until he caught it, at which point he slid a piece of paper under the glass, carried it outside, and released the fly. Spiders received the same treatment. Only mosquitoes got swatted.

My father did this because he wanted to avoid a splattered mess, and saw spiders as beneficials. But growing up, I always thought he possessed a Franciscan compassion for brother fly. I filed it alongside the line Mark had quoted from Thomas More's *Utopia*—"Every brutal act brutalizes the brutalizer"— as a reminder to avoid cruelty whenever possible. I gave up the pleasures of my younger days—squishing worms on rain-soaked sidewalks, decimating anthills, salting slugs—in an attempt to emulate what I thought was Dad's saintliness.

BUT INSIDE, I WAS UNCHANGED. My own attitude toward flies was so far from Franciscan that I once took poetic license to question God's judgment for keeping them around. Pausing one afternoon while Dad and I weeded the vegetable garden, I rhapsodized, "I wonder why / God made the fly / If I were God / I'd make them die." I started thinking that maybe flies, and almost certainly mosquitoes, were visited upon the world as a punishment for Adam's sin. Surely something so annoying would never have disturbed the peace of Eden?

Mark was quick to correct my musings, noting that God had completed His creation during the six days of Genesis. Further, He had looked upon what He had made and said it was good. Insofar as a thing was created, it had to be good, since God cannot be the cause of evil. I thought of that conversation when I read the Devil's sermon in John Updike's *The Witches of Eastwick*. In it, Satan lays out the horrific lifestyle of the tapeworm and marvels at the nastiness of any God who would create such a parasitic monster. And I thought of it on that humid D.C. evening, as I beheld my brother, prone and cursing, eyes glaring, shoe-hand cocked back.

Like Mark, I married a woman who cannot handle cockroaches. Deirdre is a splendid, practical woman, as grounded as she is witty, unfazed by the messiness of the physical world.

But when, while sweeping under the couch for a lost sandal, she brought forth a (dead) roach within a few inches of her face, she made a sound I had never heard before. Shock made her inhale, while fear made her scream. The result was a twisted, shuddering moan. Later, in a demonstration of our like-mindedness, she opined that roaches were a result of the Fall. I related to her what Mark had told me, and I saw her flirt inwardly with heresy.

More than any other creepy-crawly, God seems to have put enmity between the roach and the woman. Besides their almost essential repugnance, they bring shame on their hostess, as if Deirdre can hear them crowing, "Here is a woman whose home offers me succor, where I may take my ease amongst the filth and scum." They have a unique effect on me as well. Slugs do not bring on that tightening high in the chest. Spiders do not make my face twitch with emotion. No other varmint tempts me toward hatred.

We had always kept a clean kitchen. I grew up in a house where the men did the dishes right after dinner, and I maintained the tradition. But now, Deirdre began taking bleach to every surface—to no avail. Our house backed onto an alley, and we had roaches. Great big roaches, over an inch long, brown-black like burnt caramel, their quickness all the more unnerving because of their size.

In the beginning, they came out to die. We found them about once a week, belly up, legs folded neatly toward their middle, as if laid out in gruesome state. We found them near the fridge, next to the water dispenser, under the couch, even on the mantle. They were all dead, or nearly dead. Sometimes, they gave futile kicks with their spiny legs, or waved their long antennae in saucy defiance. I had to squish them underfoot, a messy business during which Deirdre made sure she was elsewhere. The situation wasn't quite dire enough to call the roach man. They were dying. It was never more than one at a time. It was only once in a while.

Whatever was killing them must have worn off. I caught one dallying above the hot water heater. He died in a cloud of roach spray, but he didn't go quietly. My initial blast forced him to drop to the floor; I could hear him land behind the heater. I caught him dashing for a crack in the wall. We surprised another during his nocturnal exploration of our silverware. I didn't bother with spray, just knocked him to the floor and crushed him. (I find myself using "him" instead of "it," as if cockroaches were persons, capable of moral evil.) The third Deirdre found basking in our fruit bowl—in broad daylight. I was summoned with all speed, and dispatched my enemy after a prolonged attempt to flush him out. Always, as I lunged and jabbed with my fork, I could see those antennae waving. It seemed an obscene gesture. Still, we didn't call the roach man. Until . . .

Deirdre was in the bathroom. I was in the living room. Finian was in the kitchen, all of eight months old. My parental ear, the ear that listens for portentous silence, perked up, and I looked over at my son. He was bent over something on the floor, an intent expression on his face. He was chewing. My stomach dropped. I hurtled into the kitchen, snatched up Finian, and saw the roach. It was dead, belly up. I couldn't bear to check it for missing legs.

"Fin has just finished breakfast," I thought. "He might be chewing a peach. Yes, that's it, a peach." But I knew I had to make sure. I knew I had to inspect his mouth for roach legs. And I couldn't. I stood there, holding my son at arm's length, paralyzed with fear. Fin kept chewing, his jaw set with determination. He suspected that I was going to go after his morsel. He was wrong. I was too scared. Instead, I asked, "What have you got in your mouth? Have you got a roach leg in your mouth?" As if I expected a response. Time slowed to a sickly crawl.

Deirdre had been listening to all this from the bathroom with growing alarm. After I repeated my pathetic question, the bathroom door flew open, and she charged forth. She shot me a look that let me know I was an utter failure as a father and as a man, and jammed her finger inside Fin's mouth. Deirdre, who hated and feared the roach, was not about to let any part of one get inside her son. He was chewing a peach. I called the roach man.

∽⌀∽⌀∽⌀∽⌀∽⌀

not home until we die

WE STAYED IN OUR FIRST HOUSE for two years. We moved because I wanted to be settled. I wanted to be settled so much that I had talked about living in our two-bedroom house indefinitely, cramming all our future children into eleven hundred square feet of living space and a postage-stamp yard, all for the sake of preserving that feeling of stability. I wanted to be *home*. When our second son was born, I looked at the house and the ridiculous rise in San Diego real estate prices, and decided it was time for a move. I still wanted to be settled, I just wanted to be settled in a more suitable place. We pushed into east county, looking for more bedrooms and a backyard.

The ordeal provided a good lesson in giving everything over. (It's a curious expression, "giving everything over," since all I really have to give is my will, but it feels like there's so much more that's mine.) My inability to influence the move-ments of the world was paraded in front of me again and again. Our house sold for less than we hoped—we took our agent's advice. Our first two offers on other houses—good offers, we thought—were rejected. Deirdre, who with each offer had begun to plot out the eventual improvements to our hoped-for home, had to untangle her heart from their charms. When we found the right house—a fixer-upper with four bedrooms, a quarter-acre lot, and a garage converted to a playroom—it cost, of course, more than we had hoped to pay. We were not in charge; we were floating leaves, buffeted about by number-less eddies and tides.

Life became a needling hailstorm of offers and counter-offers, repair requests and counters to those requests. It became a parade of physical inspectors, termite inspectors, appraisers, and contractors. And because we were selling one house and buying another, everything happened in duplicate. We were forever calling our agent's answering service, feeling like our whole life was not only in boxes but in boxes teetering on the edge of a cliff. *Where will we be living in six weeks? When will we know one way or the other?*

For three months, it felt like finding and buying a house was all we were doing. Other people were getting married, having children, reading books, living life. We were buying a house.

ᵔᵔᵔᵔᵔ

SAINT PAUL WROTE that he wanted Christians "to be free of anxieties," so he recommended against marrying. "The unmarried man is anxious about the affairs of the Lord, how to please the Lord; but the married man is anxious about worldly affairs, how to please his wife, and his interests are divided" (1 Corinthians 7:32–34). I was most anxious. I gave much thought to where I would lay my head.

"Whatever God wants," offered my mother, over the phone. "He will give you what is best for you." I groaned and gave my assent, then continued fretting over details. I couldn't exactly argue with her claim, but I could do my best to sidestep it. These were my children. This was my home. Except it wasn't really my home. We are not home, and will not be home until we die. In some ways, this is just a brief way station, a work camp. Not much sense in even unpacking our boxes, except that we must do so in order to make a life pleasing to God. If we are to make a good departure, we have to dig in and do what good we can, however brief our stay.

I learned a little bit about not feeling too settled and about the penetration of God into something as mundane as a termite inspection. For wherever there is temptation to sin, surely God is there as well. And there was temptation, toward a sin I hadn't really noticed in myself before—anger. When it came to sins against temperance, I was much more familiar with lust. Anger, real anger, seemed distant enough to be argued about in the abstract. Guys I knew were fond of pointing to Christ's righteous anger when he drove the money changers out of the temple. But wrath is one of the seven deadly sins for a reason. Like lust, it clouds the mind and bends the will. Judgments made in anger are rarely in keeping with the charity that bears all things and forgives all things. Like lust, it drives the self into itself, so that other people are seen only insofar as they affect the self, and not as people in their own right. This is not news, but it was news to me. I wasn't used to seething.

Two days before escrow closed and our house was sold, the buyer walked through and, possibly with the help of his agent, decided he didn't like the work we had done on the place. One issue was a two-inch crack in a floorboard. We said it was a gouge; the agent thought it looked like termite damage. The termite inspector named it a Section 1 item (incorrectly, it turned out), which meant we had to fix it. We called the termite company, and they sent a man out who put some white putty in the crack.

The agent returned and called the work "unsatisfactory." He insisted we replace the board, something we couldn't possibly do in the day remaining before the close of escrow. Our life was in boxes. Fin had broken his collarbone the night before by rolling out of bed onto a plastic crate. The movers were scheduled; the switching over of utilities was scheduled. Now it was all going south. My wife stood in the bedroom, weeping, crying at the agent, "Why are you making my life hell over this one board? I have two small children! Why are you doing this?" The agent didn't blink. He said he was protecting the interests of his client.

I wasn't there. When Deirdre told me about it, I felt my face flush with rage. *What a bastard.* But when I called Dad to tell him about it, I got no sympathy. "You have to wonder what that man is going through," advised Dad. "What difficulties must be going on in his life for him to behave that way." So simple, so basic. It's another suffering soul out there. The rage drained away. A flurry of phone calls between agents, termite inspectors, buyers, and us, and everything was better. When I gave my mother the news, I found myself turning impish once more: "It's almost as if there's a God."

⋰⋰⋰⋰⋰

I OUGHT TO CLING TO GOD when my life is upset by storms, rather than entertain tiny resentments against Him or forget about Him altogether. Any suffering, however petty, may be joined to the work of the Cross. And the trauma over house-buying *was* petty; I knew it was. I hated talking to friends about the whole thing. It seemed so material, so bound up with the world as to make my attention to it shameful.

God is spirit, but the world, as Hopkins told us, is charged with His grandeur, and He insinuates Himself into the most material aspects of creation. He sanctifies the fleshy union of sex, making it an occasion of grace. He even ties himself up with filthy lucre, and upon consideration, this is not surprising. Money is deeply connected to the spiritual life, for it forms a quick and powerful attachment to the will. Love of money is called the root of all evil because money is often the first agent of self-gratification. My friend Jon told me that when he read in Scripture that the giving of alms is efficacious for the removal of sin, it felt to him like a revelation. You can't buy your way into heaven, but you can perhaps spend (or hoard) your way into hell. And if money wasn't too material for God, neither was the house. Only the anxiety was shameful.

Moving into the new house brought a lot of joys, but didn't ease my anxiety. It only shifted the focus. I was in, but my big new house scared me. I wanted this to be the family manse; would I be able to keep up the payments? And when I had filled those empty bedrooms with children, what would that cost me, financially and otherwise? "The Lord will take care," consoled my mother, but why should He? My college chaplain, Father Steckler, once told the story of a woman who had nine children, four of whom left the church. "And she was a great saint, so don't be surprised if it happens to you," he warned, grinning that wicked grin.

A sign that we are meant for heaven: we expect happiness. We expect things to be perfect. This doesn't make much sense, since imperfection surrounds us always. Why should we expect anything else? But we do. We complain naturally, without effort. We must be taught to count our blessings.

It's a hard thing to learn, counting one's blessings. For one thing, I must overcome the tendency to think that what is familiar is what is normal, that the level of comfort and well-being that has surrounded me in my own life is just the way things are. Abstractly, of course, I know this is non-sense. I have been wildly fortunate. Happily married parents who loved me, good education, good job, decent health, the goods of wife and family—the list is long, and is capped by the great gift of faith. But when I am downhearted, when I am under the yoke of suffering, the list provides shockingly little consolation.

Blessings are from the Lord. It is hard to remember that the sufferings—my little ones and the great ones of others—are from the Lord as well. (My father is fond of repeating this thought from Father Peter Gabriel, author of *Divine Intimacy*:

"All [sufferings], even the tiniest, have been predisposed by God from all eternity for our sanctification" [Father Gabriel of St. Mary Magdalene, O.C.D., *Divine Intimacy: Meditations on the Interior Life for Every Day of the Liturgical Year* {Rockford, IL: Tan Books and Publishers, Inc., 1964}, 381].) I am not so mired in earth as to suppose that those who suffer greatly are being punished for their sins, or that they are outside the circle of the Lord's chosen. Nor do I suppose that the prosperous are beloved by God. But I still associate earthly happiness with grace, still hope that if I remain as faithful as I can, my life will be free of calamity. I will not lose my job, will not lose my home, will not contract a terrible disease. In short, I will not suffer the fate of God's upright servant Job.

THIS IS PATENTLY SILLY, as I was recently reminded. A young woman I know with two small children and a third on the way, a woman who radiated strength and vitality, was diagnosed with leukemia. She lost the baby in her womb, and for a time, we thought she might lose her life. After my initial rush of pity and concern, self-love led me to imagine being in such a position, and then to imagine being in the position of her husband, facing the prospect of working and raising two kids without a mother. Good Lord.

First, there is the childlike faith that all will be well. Then, after a little suffering and a little insight, the certainty that all cannot possibly be well. Then, after a little reflection, the conscious reliance on grace to ensure that all will be well. And finally, Lord willing, the true knowledge that whatever comes, however awful, all things work together for good for those that love God. Anything less is naïveté, rightly subject to the mockery of the unbeliever: "He committed his cause to the LORD; let him deliver him, let him rescue him, for he delights in him!" (Psalm 22:8).

෨ ෨ ෨ ෨ ෨

boy meets god

IN HIGH SCHOOL, before my friend Steven and I gave up arguing about things like God and abortion, he told me he was grateful that his father had let him make his own decisions about religious belief. (He had decided against it.)

It's not as if *my* father put a gun to my head and asked me to recite the Creed, or let me know that there wouldn't be any atheists sleeping under his Catholic roof. But I see Steven's point. Dad did tell me the faith was true, and he was Dad, a position that wields a lot of influence. A child tends to believe a father.

Faith is personal. You can't believe just because somebody else does, even if that somebody is your father. But a father has care for his children. If God exists, then there is nothing more important to teach your children than the truth of that existence. If you can't actually impart the gift of faith, you can do an awful lot to dispose the soul to receive it. And I fully expect my own final judgment to include an accounting of my efforts to pass along what I have received by word and example. My kids are the first objects of my obligation to go out and teach all nations.

I didn't have to make the first step—"Fin, it's time you learned about Jesus." Like any kid, Fin was asking questions soon after he learned to talk. At four, he lobbed this one at Deirdre from the backseat of the car—"Why do I do bad things that I don't want to do?" And there was my wife, smack dab at the heart of the Christian faith we promised to teach: fallen man in need of redemption. Deirdre was impressed: What a sharp, introspective kid! Then she was nervous: *Here we go . . .*

How would I have answered? At the time, I imagined myself telling my boy the story of Adam and Eve, feeling just a tad silly as I did so. "Talking snakes!" Fin would have been fascinated and triumphant. I was always telling him that animals can't really talk the way they do in cartoons. I imagined telling him that, just as he has inherited certain facial features from me, he has inherited a fallen nature from his first father, a nature that tends toward naughtiness and is susceptible to temptation.

After a while, imagination gave way to reality, and I have been surprised at the amount of resentment Fin shows toward Adam and Eve. It never occurred to me to wish that they had not sinned. "*Why* did she have to take the apple?" he cries after some failure of goodwill on his part. "If she hadn't, then none of this would have happened!"

My son is quick to look outside himself like that. From my teaching that God made everything and that everything exists only because God wants it to, four-year-old Fin jumped to the idea that God makes him do bad things. This came partly from the fact that when he misbehaves, I often ask him why he has done what he has done. I want him to understand himself, but he wants to look elsewhere.

"No," I countered, defending God. "God is good and does not make anyone do anything that is not good. Temptations toward evil are from the devil."

"Then the devil made me do it!"

"No, the devil can only tempt you."

"Then my temptations made me do it!"

"No, you can resist your temptations. Ask God for help."

That led to more trouble. Why, he wondered, did he continue to fail even after asking for help?

"Why does God give me temptations?" He was angry now, red-faced and throwing himself on his bed. "Stop giving me temptations, God!"

He sensed that God remains the ultimate source of things. God, after all, allows the tempter to exist.

HIS QUESTIONS gave rise to my own. Who tempted the tempter? Did God give that first temptation, the one that lured Lucifer to fall? He made everything that is, and He is goodness itself, so everything that is must be good. Evil, says St. Augustine, comes from a "deficient cause," a sort of hole in being. The common answer to the question, "Why is there evil?" is "Because there is free will." But whence came the desire to turn from the face of the Almighty? What greater good presented itself? Lucifer's will was not damaged at his creation as ours is, nor was his intellect darkened. He saw God for what He was, and what was more, he was God's favorite. What happened?

My son liked the idea that there will be no more temptations in heaven, but otherwise, he didn't want to go there. He couldn't imagine happiness away from home, from the house we lived in at the time. He kept asking, "But will we get to come back to this house?" The house was crucial for him. After we had gone 'round about this for a while, he announced with obvious pleasure that he didn't need to go to heaven, because he had God in the house: "He's hanging on the cross on the wall." This despite numerous explanations that Jesus is no longer on the cross, that we have the crucifix in the house to remind us of how much He loved us.

I pulled my mother's old trick: "If you want to come to our house when you're in heaven, you will." This is true in one way; our heart's desires *will* be met in heaven. But he was not satisfied with my answer; he sensed the fudging. Nor was he satisfied with the straight truth, that maybe heaven would be so wonderful that he wouldn't want to come back here.

A smattering of Finian's spiritual life at four: He said his prayers at night and grace before meals. He liked the stories in the *Catholic Children's Treasure Box*, a sweetly old-fashioned children's publication, about little Thérèse offering gifts for God. He imitated me and said Hail Marys when he saw an ambulance, asking our Lady's assistance for the person inside. He asked about God all the time—His size, what He could and could not do, how He could know everything.

By five, I was seeing my own sins reflected in his soul, wondering how much I had passed on to him. Fin was a sensualist, licking his lips as he talked of sweets and professing a desire to "marry all the girls" so he could "have them." He was forever desiring, allowing lust for stuff to dictate his behavior in all sorts of unpleasant ways, particularly ingratitude. As soon as one desire was satisfied, he was on to the next thing, asking to go somewhere even as we arrived home from somewhere else. His temper was short, and he gave in to shouting at his brother when he was offended. He was easily frustrated and allowed that frustration to carry him away, past the most obvious solutions. (In his case, asking a parent for help; in mine, asking God.) I will not say I caused these habits entirely, but surely some of his readiness to indulge them came from watching me.

As bad as I am, I don't think I ever disliked Sundays (read: attending Mass) as intensely as he did then. The scene was played out almost every week: On entering his room to get dressed after his bath, he saw that his church clothes had been laid out, and he began to look like someone had stolen all his toys. Though he knew his misery would displease me, and though he did not want to displease me, he couldn't help himself: "I have to say, I don't like Sundays," he lamented. "Why do we have to go to church?"

Why? Because God commanded that we keep holy the Sabbath. Actually, I never used that one. When I was Fin's age, my own reason for going was far less remote: I went because my parents went. That was that. Later, I went because the church, God's voice on earth, required it. Now, on a personal level, I go to receive the Eucharist and so be strengthened and transformed. But it was the church's rule that created my habit of getting there every week, whether I received or not.

Fin was not old enough to receive the Eucharist, so I couldn't point to that. And though we told him we were eating Jesus' body and drinking His blood, I don't think it really registered. When something curious hit home, he asked about it. He never asked about eating God.

I never used the "God commanded it" line in part because it's not my reason, and in part because I don't want to make God into the heavy. But I got tripped up on the line I did take: "Because God has given us everything we have, and we need to say thank you, and going to church is how we thank Him." When Fin persisted in his protests—"Why do we have to thank Him *in church*?"—his dad, rushed as he often was, trying to cram children's feet into stiff leather church shoes, got testy. Dad started hauling out the charge of ingratitude. Sometimes, Dad snapped. "Should we just take away all your toys, since you don't want to say thank you?" And bingo, God was the heavy—to say nothing of Dad. I might have been better off resorting to the command. Fin understands commands, understands that I have authority, and that God has more authority still.

(It's not that Fin is a bad kid. He's a good kid: tough, smart, strong willed. If he thinks he's right about something, he won't back down until he's sure we understand him completely. If he sees he's wrong, he'll admit it, even if it's clear everything in him wants to rebel. His memory is astonishing: once he picks up a principle, it stays. He strives to overcome his faults, to let us know he's trying: "Mom, I'm not being passive-aggressive here, but . . ." And all this is just in the moral realm; my considerations here do not touch on his creativity, his dexterous handling of language, his thoughtfulness, his care for his younger siblings. He's a wonder to me, my first-born son.)

HERE WAS THE PROBLEM: religion didn't matter much to five-year-old Fin. Religion is concerned with satisfying the deepest longings of the human heart, longings he couldn't even identify yet. He thought the blessings of family, friends, and stuff were pretty great, and more stuff and more friends would be even greater.

Religion gave a reason for behaving, but his parents provided motivation enough for that. Religion pointed to the fate of the soul in the life after this one, another thing that didn't hold much interest for Fin. I didn't talk much about the possibility of separation from God. It wasn't really a danger for him yet, and I didn't want him to cling to Christ out of fear. With hell out of the picture, heaven didn't sound all that appealing to him, except for the possibility of doing whatever he wanted.

"I could eat ice cream all day," he marveled, grinning at the thought of such transgressive indulgence.

"True," we told him, "but you won't want anything that's bad for you." That killed his buzz a little.

A person might be tempted to ease up on the religious talk. He's a good kid, not really culpable for his sins, and unable to appreciate a lot of what I'm saying. Why push it?

Why? Because the habits are already forming. When I see his materialism, his conviction that the next thing he gets will bring him true satisfaction (and the next, and the next, and the next), I see the longing that can be filled by love alone. When I run up against his fierce desire for independence, I see an instinctive resistance to authority. These are habits that may well affect his religious experience. They demand attention.

My son revealed my limitations. There is a beauty, a romance, a desirability to the faith—it is, after all, an encounter with *love* itself. I see that beauty, sometimes more clearly than others, but I was unable to communicate it to the boy. And he wasn't interested in the glories of the faith. He was more interested in asking, "What can't God do?" I should have answered scholastically: "God cannot lie or do evil." But I didn't. I said, "He can't live in the heart of someone who has rejected Him." Finian smiled, seemingly pleased at the thought of defeating God.

Now, at seven, his temperament is more and more his own. "Dad, I wish you didn't write about wine," he said one day. "I wish you wrote about guns and technology."

That's Fin all over, especially the technology part. He's a tremendous materialist. If I point out a bad habit, he blames it on a disconnected wire in his brain. If only he could connect the wire, the habit would disappear. Even his remorse has a material character.

"Sorry."

"Come on. Say it like you mean it."

"I didn't know I had to actually *be* sorry. I thought I just had to *say* it."

It's the same with prayers. He says them willingly enough every night and at Mass, but he admits with disarming honesty that he doesn't really mean the words. He's a great one for the exterior forms; his younger brother Isaac is our interior boy. Ask Fin to do a job and he does it. Isaac's likely to lose steam after a minute or two. But Isaac does volunteer work. "I want to set the table because I love you, and it makes you happy."

Isaac talks more about love in general. "Dad, even when you're mad at us, you still love us. Just like God loves us." When Isaac assured me that he loved God more than anything, Fin was moved to confess, "Dad, *I* don't really love God more than anything. I think I love Mom more than I love God."

"It's hard for you to love God, because you don't see Him, is that it?"

"Yes."

Fin wants experience. Isaac is more credulous. Isaac was discussing God with my mother:

"God went into the water and made the sea creatures?"

"God didn't have to go into the water; he made the water, too."

"He used magic?"

"Well, not exactly. God doesn't really use magic."

"The *priest* uses magic."

"The priest uses magic? What does he use magic for?"

Isaac looked at her as if the answer couldn't be plainer. "To defeat the devil!"

My sister-in-law Lisa joined in. "It's the power of God."

"The priest uses the power *with* God."

"You're going to be a priest, Isaac," said Lisa.

Finian, on the other hand, doesn't want to be a priest. He wants to be married. He wants love like the love between

Deirdre and me. He wants children to command. He wants the world he knows, the world he has experienced.

How much of the difference is because of me? By the time Isaac came along, I was explaining myself more. "I cannot allow you to behave badly. I love you, and I want you to be happy. You won't be happy if you're not good. So I have to help you be good." Is that why he talks about love, love that persists even in anger? When Fin shows signs of hardness or indifference toward the feelings of others, is that because he sometimes found me unsympathetic as I disciplined him? Was I, am I too hard?

"Our Fathers were our models for God," says Tyler Durden in the movie *Fight Club*. I try to explain to my children that I am not God, that God is perfect and I am not. I apologize to them when I lose my temper or act unjustly. But I see my influence, good and bad. Raising kids is an awesome task. Who can shoulder it? I love them so much, and worry about the men and women they will become. I'm doing my best. I hope my best will improve. I will try to improve it.

Meanwhile, the children change like water. Fin, my exterior-forms man, wrote a prayer during Mass recently: "Lord, I love you. I will try to serve you well. I'm sorry for what I have done wrong. Jesus, help me to detach from stuff. I will be good. Amen." Thank God for God.

∾∾∾∾∾

PART III

WISE AS SERPENTS

∾∾∾∾∾

ぶぶぶぶ

alms for a drink

IT'S ODD WHAT LODGES IN THE MEMORY; why this and not that? In particular, why do I remember fights better than anything else? My wife forgets them completely. I'll bring up what I thought to be a watershed moment in our relationship, a time when heated conflict brought some long-simmering issue to a proper boil, and all I'll get is an intrigued raising of the eyebrows—"Really? That happened? Hm."

A fight—or rather, a brief skirmish following a surprise attack—also provides one of my clearest memories of Cara, the first girl I ever loved. We were fifteen when our affair began, sixteen when it ended. Our romance was forever threatening to eat itself. We talked about the relationship more than we talked about anything else, and the closed-off quality only heightened the emotional intensity.

This particular exchange took place in late fall of our junior year, on an afternoon when I took Cara to hang out on the Ithaca Commons. As Cara and I sat outside and talked, a disheveled man sidled up to us and asked for some money for food. I reached into my pocket. My father had told me that he used to wonder about giving money to street people, but he ceased his wondering when he read Jesus' unqualified exhortation in the Sermon on the Mount: "Give to every one who begs from you" (Luke 6:30). After that, every time I was petitioned, His words (with Dad's voice) sounded in my head.

My pocket yielded no change, so I gave the man a dollar bill. I was careful to say, "God bless you," instead of "good luck" as I did so. I wanted the man to understand my motivations. I wanted him to understand that God was the real source of generosity. As the man walked away, my girlfriend said, with palpable disappointment, "You just bought that man his next drink."

Stung, I got defensive. I was surprised to hear criticism coming from what I thought would be a sympathetic corner—Cara was a Methodist and serious about her Christianity.

"You don't know that," I retorted. "And besides, so what if I did? Maybe that drink is his only comfort in life." The sharpness of my reply was fueled by wounded pride, and by a sneaking suspicion that she may have been right to criticize me. Surely I was not really in favor of a man blowing whatever money he could scrounge up on booze?

And yet, Jesus said, "Give to the man who begs from you." Surely He knew the nature of those beggars—that some would spend their alms on whatever would, if only for a moment, relieve their suffering? I'm not a literalist; I do not handle poisonous serpents. And I'm not asking, "What would Jesus do?" I'm asking, "What would Jesus have *me* do?" What is the prudent thing to do in the face of another's need?

჻჻჻჻჻

A FEW YEARS AGO, I got to ask that question in earnest. What was the prudent thing to do with Sabrina? Sabrina was homeless, bone-thin, begging at a busy intersection for herself and her two children. The children, she said, were with a friend. My wife, Deirdre, had been asked to write a newspaper story about a homeless woman, and so she interviewed Sabrina about her life and how she had got where she was. Needless to say, it was a heart-wrenching story. After they talked, Deirdre gave Sabrina forty dollars for a motel that night—the interview had taken prime begging time. Feeling moved to generosity, Deirdre also gave her a business card that included our home phone number.

Gradually, we were drawn into the unholy mess of her life: the parents who allegedly hated her and had kicked her out, the unemployed boyfriend (and father of her children) who couldn't seem to catch a break, the friends who agreed to help if she put a little money up front.

The calls became more frequent. Every time Sabrina called and I heard Deirdre tell her, "I'll have to talk to my husband," my heart sank. What advice could I give? When is it enough? Jesus never said when to stop. He talked about walking the extra mile, giving from your want. This woman kept coming to us in seeming desperation. After a couple of months, we had given her over five hundred dollars. I talk about consulting the Holy Spirit, but I am rotten at discernment. I ask with utter sincerity for guidance, but always end up following what feels more like gut instinct or reasoned conclusion than any spiritual stirring. When it comes to almsgiving, I go back to my father's example.

We got up in the middle of the night to go down to Sabrina's motel and pay the bill. We drove the boyfriend, Jason, to the women's prison when Sabrina was arrested for I don't remember what. I wrote a letter to Jason encouraging him to be a man and be a father; he broke down and wept when he told me how much he appreciated it.

IN THE END, we discovered that Sabrina had lied to us again and again, principally about needing money in order to care for her two children. Both had long since been taken from her by the courts. We discovered that she had not sought out homeless shelters because she didn't want to sleep apart from her boyfriend, who would not be allowed to live with her. We discovered lots of reasons to suspect that Sabrina was addicted to drugs, lying with incredible dexterity in an effort to keep her habit funded. We felt betrayed. Worse, we felt we were helping her perpetuate her misery. She had skipped appointments we set up with social workers, failed to apply for homeless shelters—because she could count on us to bail her out. We finally broke off the relationship. She left an angry, vaguely threatening message on our machine; she said we should have known she was lying, and that we had just used her for the newspaper story.

Our last contact with her was another message, this one chillling instead of threatening. She had managed to get pregnant again, and so would be able to collect benefits from the government. We said a prayer, for her and for the child.

With Sabrina, I had cause to say no, and I steeled myself against her. But mostly, I am a sensitive (soft?) man. Most often, when a man (or woman) asks me for money, I think not of his laziness or his questionable story or his evil habits, but of the suffering that has driven him to this humiliation. I think of the abuse he must suffer from those who see him as a blight and let him know it. I think of his crippled spirit, and unless I smell booze on him (Why not then?), I give something. I feel as if he has made himself vulnerable, and that vulnerability sets up an intimacy, and in that intimacy, I am more likely to see another suffering member of the body of Christ. It's too much; I cannot back away.

୬୬୬୬୬

pop goes the hymnal

THE MASS HAS ALWAYS BEEN the center of my faith. But where to go to Mass? Growing up in Cortland, I went to St. Mary's, because that's where my parents went. It never occurred to me to go elsewhere, even if there were things about St. Mary's that didn't thrill me. Things like the music.

Though certain of my friends rib me for being old before my time—indulging in a crotchety rejection of the active and varied joys of youth in favor of the sedentary and regular pleasures of age—I am still a young man. I did not suffer what must have been the wrenching shift from the Tridentine rite to the current order of Mass. I cannot look back fondly on "the good old days," and certainly not on "the good old hymns." Outside of Handel's *Messiah*, I did not hear ancient or classical sacred choral music until I went to college. I am a *Glory and Praise* baby, a member of the generation raised on "Here I Am," "Though the Mountains May Fall," and "Be Not Afraid."

How to explain, then, my untaught antipathy for the hymns of my youth, especially when those hymns so clearly sought to please the young? Many were based on the wonderful words of the Psalms, but the music seemed to somehow change the meaning. The guitars, the syncopation, the folksy melodies; they all mirrored, in a sad, "spiritualized" way, the pop music of the 1960s and beyond. I liked pop music; I still do. I grew up on show tunes, doing dinner dishes while singing along to the original cast recordings of *Camelot*, *My Fair Lady*, *Guys and Dolls*, and any number of others. I fell in love with The Beatles, and later, with R.E.M., U2, and They Might Be Giants. But those hymns weren't good pop, and they weren't good church music. They were a mushy amalgamation of the two that resulted in something less than either.

The sound of those hymns was sentimental, but sappily, not touchingly so. "Amazing Grace"—now there was touching sentiment. There was genuine folk. "Were You There"? Same thing. But "Blest Be the Lord"? Even if the thoughts expressed by the lyrics were true as could be and straight out of the tradition, the songs felt contrived. "We're going to get some contemporary sounds in here, yes sir!" They were, I decided as a teenager, silly. I still think so today.

Part of that silliness came from the wild incongruity of it: the strumming guitars and electronic synthesizer echoing in the Gothic grandeur of the church, the trippy tunes thundering forth from the pipe organ, the wizened old women in the congregation straining their voices after sentimental ballads like "On Eagle's Wings" or peppy anthems like "Lord of the Dance." The music was crowbarred into the life of the congregation, even though it had nothing to do with them. Our parish was full of aging, reserved Irish. Why make them sing like kids? What did it signify? What good effect was intended?

One *bad* effect, intended or not, was the shift away from music as a prayerful sound, floating overhead toward the altar, disposing the soul to contemplate the Lord we had gathered to meet. Music became an opportunity for performers to show their stuff. I remember the first time I saw choir steps in the sanctuary at St. Mary's. I remember the first time I saw a drum set and amplifiers, at my grandparents' church in Florida. "Who needs a choir loft? We've got a stage right up front!" These days, the congregation often applauds at the end of the "performance." Whatever the intentions of the performers, the music commands more attention than it ought to. Gone are the days when my mother told me to exit the church quietly, out of reverence for the Blessed Sacrament in the tabernacle. Gone, from the sanctuary of St. Mary's, is the tabernacle.

I still sang. (I still do.) I sang because I believed that participation is good, even if it is not pleasant. But my belief led to another problem, this one a matter of timing: I try to consider my sins prior to communion, so that I am able, in the words of St. Thomas Aquinas, to "receive the bread of angels, the King of kings, the Lord of lords, with such reverence and humility, such contrition and devotion, such purity and faith, such purpose and intention, as may tend to the salvation of my soul." As I work at recollection and repentance, I am almost always interrupted by the voice from the speaker—"The communion hymn will be number 379, 'One Bread, One Body.' We will sing verses 1, 3, and 5."

For years, I was undecided. Should I join in the communion hymn, singing, as some did, as I approached the altar? Or should I stay within myself, thinking about my sins, about the sacrament, about my soul? Finally, I determined that my contribution to the voice of the community was not needed at that point in the Mass. I held my tongue and kept it held after receiving, choosing instead to pray to the God I had just consumed.

How to explain my early love for "old" hymns, though I did not yet recognize them as old? Every Holy Thursday, as the monstrance was paraded around the church after the evening Mass, I sank into the sweet strains of the *Pange Lingua* and I wondered why we didn't sing this lovely, haunting hymn often.

> *Down in adoration falling*
> *This great sacrament we hail,*
> *Over ancient forms of worship*
> *Newer rites of grace prevail;*
> *Faith will tell us Christ is present*
> *When our human senses fail.*

And though I understood why the jubilant "Jesus Christ is Risen Today" was reserved for Easter Sunday Mass, I longed for more hymns like it. I loved hymns you could belt out, hymns that filled your chest as you sang them, hymns full of quarter notes and easy intervals, well suited to large, untrained choirs. Hymns like "Holy Holy Holy," "Come Holy Ghost," "Praise to the Lord." Hymns full of glory and majesty and power. Music goes straight to my gut and straight to my soul. It is the quickest way to elicit from me an interior response. It stirs my spirit, for good or ill. There's an overused but still accurate word for the effect of the good stuff—uplifting. Tender or passionate or powerful, it's still uplifting. That's what I need out of my hymns.

ɔ̸ɒ̸ɔ̸ɒ̸ɔ̸

in which we go parish hopping

THE DAY I INTERVIEWED for my job at the *Reader*, I stopped in at Our Lady of the Rosary Church, one block from the paper's offices in San Diego's Little Italy. As I thanked our Lady (and Pappy) for helping me find employment, I marveled that a place could be so quiet and yet so busy. The entire interior— walls, windows, arched ceiling, front corners, back corners, sanctuary, choir loft—was bursting with devotional art. A crowded crucifixion spread out across the front, the throngs at the judgment across the back. It was like the old European churches I had heard about, where the pictures could preach the homily. I was used to the relative restraint of my northeastern Gothic—no painted statues, thank you, white marble will do—but this church had the advantage of proximity, since I would be spending the next few months in a nearby hotel.

Later, I discovered that the church also had daily Mass at noon, said by one of its two Italian Barnabite priests, Father

Louis. Father Louis was exuberant. His sermons hopped around like rabbits, darting from point to point, pausing occasionally to take stock, then plunging ahead. When he was up on the altar, age had nothing to do with him; it was only when you got up close that you saw the effects of time. He was my first magnetic priest—the attraction he engendered was a dynamic force.

When I moved to Hillcrest, my apartment probably fell into the parish borders of St. John the Evangelist. The Spanish love nest I found with Deirdre most likely belonged to St. Vincent de Paul, and our first house to St. Didacus. But through all those moves, we kept attending Our Lady of the Rosary. We loved Father Louis. We could tell that Father Louis loved Jesus, and we could tell he loved us, his brothers and sisters in the congregation.

Father wasn't strict with the language of the Mass. Most famously, he appended "parents, teachers, teenagers" to the phrase "all the people you have gained" in the Eucharistic Prayer. But it didn't bother me the way it bothered me when Father Frank altered the Mass back in Cortland. First, Father Louis wasn't changing the words of the consecration, the words that actually effected the transformation of bread and wine into Body and Blood. Second, the spirit behind the changes seemed different. When Father Louis held the Host aloft and proclaimed, "This is *Jesus*, the Lamb of God, who takes away the sins of the world," I felt that he added "This is Jesus" to emphasize the true presence of Christ in the Eucharist. Still, the double standard is not lost on me, and I sympathized when a friend said that one reason for fixed language is it eliminates the reliance on something so difficult to regulate and judge as "the spirit behind the changes."

But if Father Louis loved his brothers and sisters in the pews—my sinful self included—I had trouble following his lead. I had been raised to pay attention to the proceedings on the altar: listening to the priest, making the responses, joining Father in his offering of the sacrifice. You didn't even turn around to look at the choir in the back of the church. Anything less would be irreverent to God and disrespectful to the priest, not to mention your fellow worshippers, who were trying to pay attention. And if you were late to Mass, you slipped in as unobtrusively as possible.

It was different at Our Lady of the Rosary. It seemed that every week, at least one family arrived late and marched to the front of the church to find seats, sometimes during Father Louis's homily. As they shuffled their way into the pews, they exchanged grinning handshakes with their neighbors. "Hi, how ya doin'? Great to see you!" All while Father gave his sermon less than twenty feet away. I fumed. Other people waved and chatted as they made their way back from communion, the Host barely off their tongues. I couldn't stand it. I was more easily distracted and quicker to take offense than I am now. Every Sunday, I struggled against uncharitable judgments.

When we bought our first house, we found ourselves some distance from Little Italy, and much nearer to City Heights and the pink bell tower of Our Lady of the Sacred Heart. An old friend of the family paid Deirdre a visit; she told us about the parish. "You mean you've never been? You live right near it. They've got a wonderful priest, Father Rich. When he came in, he put the crucifix back over the altar." (The previous pastor had replaced it with a Risen Christ, which Father Rich moved to a side altar.) "He put the tabernacle back in the sanctuary," making it once more the focal point of the building.

It was his moving the tabernacle that made us curious to visit. We were forever hearing of churches being renovated, their tabernacles—where God himself resided in the form of consecrated Hosts—moved to a side altar or a separate room. This was the first time we'd ever heard of one being returned to the sanctuary. Who was this priest?

The church itself delighted us. The plaster-and-paint interior dated it from the 1940s, but in many ways, it reminded me of the older churches back east. High-arched ceilings, white

marble saints' statues along the sides, a great domed baldachin
over the altar. I suspect that when Father restored the crucifix
to its original place, hanging from that baldachin, he did it for
theological reasons. I suspect he wanted to keep the sacrificial
Christ, the one who suffered for love of us, in the mind of the
congregation. That would have suited him. Years later, when
I mentioned Father Rich to the old monsignor, he replied,
"Before Rich was a priest, he was a physical therapist. That's
the way he is—'Now, this will hurt.'"

Even if he hadn't been interested in theology, Father could have
replaced the crucifix for reasons of pure aesthetics. The crucifix—
a white marble corpus against a reddish-black marble cross—was
of a piece with the baldachin. The risen Christ—his leaping form
carved from wood, his appearance a study in pastels—must have
been wildly out of place hanging there, a testament to the ugliness
that blinkered theory can inflict upon coherent beauty.

We attended Mass, and I liked Father Rich immediately.
He wasn't charmingly contrarian like Father Steckler or
magnetic like Father Louis. But he was sharp minded, and
unapologetically direct in his defense of the faith and church
teaching. He was the first priest I had ever seen read from the
Catechism during a homily. He was well-read, and careful in
his speech—every condemnation of sin was accompanied by
a reminder of the love we owed the sinner. He was willing to

stand by the hard teachings, such as the church's claim that homosexual sex was fundamentally disordered. But he wasn't about to proclaim the teaching and then bar the church doors. He reached out. He was the driving force behind the local chapter of Courage, a Catholic organization devoted to helping "persons with same-sex attractions develop a life of interior chastity in union with Christ." I think he got responses.

I WAS GLAD to hear Father reaching out. When he talked of loving somebody and yet still insisting that they conform to the truth of human sexuality, he didn't come across as hateful or condemning, and he didn't leave any room for those reactions in the hearts of the faithful. Rather, he spoke with conviction untainted by condescension. And since he had embraced celibacy himself, he had credibility. It was as if he had said, "I have made this sacrifice for Christ. It is worthwhile, and it can be done."

Deirdre and I joined the parish at Our Lady of the Sacred Heart. Father Rich seemed a man after our own hearts. Though he was younger than most priests, he shared our love for the old things we so rarely saw. It wasn't nostalgia; it was an appreciation of tradition. Soon after we joined, he started a fundraising drive for new, hardback hymnals. In addition to the standard *Glory and Praise* fare, the new hymnals would include an extensive collection of older material, much of which I had never heard before. Father explained his reasons for seeking out the old hymns, and the parish responded.

Father Rich believed in "smells and bells" liturgy, and I was grateful for the old-fashioned concrete reminders of what we were about at Mass. Altar servers surrounded the altar with fragrant smoke from a silver thurible on a chain before the liturgy of the Eucharist. Father used the long Roman Canon for his Eucharistic Prayer, the one that asks God to "look with favor on these offerings and accept them as once you accepted the gifts of your servant Abel, the sacrifice of Abraham, our father in faith, and the bread and wine offered by your priest Melchisedech." These references to particular, historical figures drew me in, grounded me in the goings on, just like those I later loved in the Tridentine rite.

What was more, Father often intoned the Canon, his raspy voice taking on richness and power—this was not ordinary speech. At the elevation following the consecration, the servers rang the bells loud and strong—pay attention, people, the holy sacrifice has just been re-presented. Your God is on the altar. Like Father Frank, Father Rich was something of a showman. Unlike Father Frank, he kept his showmanship within the rubrics of the Mass.

When my attention slipped—and it always did—I could latch on to tangible reminders of God and his saints: the statues, the stained-glass windows, the dove carved in relief on the baldachin, the crucifix. I found them sympathetic the way the Eucharist is sympathetic; they acknowledged the power and immediacy of the incarnate.

After Mass, Deirdre and I brought the kids over to the side altar, where Joseph stood next to Mary, and Mary cradled the baby Jesus. Then we said a prayer to St. Joseph, placing all our earthly cares before him. We said the Our Father, the Hail Mary, and the Glory Be—outside of grace at mealtimes, it was the only time all week our entire family prayed together.

I loved Our Lady of the Sacred Heart Church, Father Rich, and the Associate Pastor, Father Phien. Father Phien was Vietnamese. Where Father Rich was explanatory and full of exhortation, Father Phien was simple, holy, and affecting. But however much I loved the priests and liturgy, in some sense, I felt like an outsider. Masses at the parish were offered in three languages: Vietnamese, Spanish, and English. Though English got the traditional 10:00 a.m. slot, it was peopled largely by Vietnamese and Hispanics, along with a smattering of African Americans and elderly whites.

I once ended up at the Vietnamese Mass on Holy Thursday by mistake. The Mass was wonderful to behold. Five minutes before the priest entered the church, the entire congregation stood, turned to the shrine of the 117 Vietnamese martyrs, bowed, and chanted in unison until Mass began. Small children, punked-out teenagers, middle-aged men—all bowing and chanting. When it came time for the washing of the feet, twelve elderly men in blue satin robes entered the sanctuary for the ceremony. I thought of the sad variations on foot-washing I had seen and heard about—an endless procession of kids heading up to get their turn, dirt-blackened bowls in which the faithful were supposed to wash each other's *hands*—and marveled at these elders' quiet dignity. But I was a spectator. Though this was my faith, it was not my culture.

My sort—younger, white, multiple small children in tow— barely registered. People were friendly toward us but not outgoing. This was their home parish; I was a transplant from another neighborhood. Without even thinking about it, I had gone parish hopping.

ᗣᗧᗣᗧᗣ

MY FRIEND ERNIE tells a remarkable story about his father. One Sunday, after hearing one too many heresies from the pulpit and enduring one too many affronts to the ritual of the Mass, Dad snapped and proceeded to drag Ernie and a number of his siblings from Mass to Mass, searching for a service that would not offend.

Such behavior was not as ready an option for my own father. We already attended the less problematic of the two Catholic churches in my hometown. I suppose we could have gone back to the Newman Center, but escape wasn't my father's style. He has an earnest, principled streak in him, a zeal for the common good. He is a writer of sincere, thoughtful letters, the kind that start by affirming the opposition's achievements and goodwill before suggesting that there is a problem. When there *is* a problem, he stays put and wages a gentle war.

Our parish priest, speaking of children about to be baptized, once said, "Someday Jesus will also say to them, 'This day you will be with me in paradise.'" My father wrote him a letter, thanking him for his "recurring reminders that we will be accountable to God for our actions and that there is no greater foolishness than to live this life without preparing for the next." Then he went on to express his surprise, in the light of these reminders, at Father's apparent assumption that the babies would eventually go to heaven. He noted that the parish's funerals made similar assumptions, inviting people to take comfort in knowing that the deceased was with the Lord now. He pointed out, in the least combative way, that this was inconsistent with the church's teaching on purgatory, and what was more, deprived the deceased of the benefit of intercessory prayer. Father didn't respond, but he stopped speaking of how a person was now "with God."

I suppose my father's example was why I found myself taking sides against my girlfriend back in college, arguing that parish hopping was a dangerous, if not uncharitable, practice. To me, it smacked of the same insularity as the notion that we Catholics need to pull away from the rest of the fallen world for fear of what it might do to us—hardly in step with the command to "go out and teach all nations." If the "good" Catholics kept to their own kind, how would the "bad" Catholics ever get brought 'round? Charity, I argued, demanded that we stay put and fight the good fight. The parish was a community; concern for the common good should be put above our own particular wishes.

At one point in C. S. Lewis's *The Screwtape Letters*, the devil Screwtape instructs his apprentice Wormwood by saying, "Surely you know that if a man can't be cured of churchgoing, the next best thing is to send him all over the neighborhood looking for a church that 'suits' him until he becomes a taster or connoisseur of churches" (*The Best of C. S. Lewis* [New York: The Iverson Associates, 1969], 60). Screwtape points to the diabolical delight in faction and in putting a critical spirit in place of a docile one. The point found its mark; I winced at the sting of recognition. Hadn't my critical spirit toward the parishioners at Our Lady of the Rosary helped land us at Our Lady of the Sacred Heart? Hadn't I become a "connoisseur of churches"?

But what if our wishes had to do with the nourishment of our souls? Wasn't that why I had parish hopped? To attend a Mass that wouldn't assault my peace of soul? To be nourished on sound doctrine as well as the body of Christ? To have my will disposed to God by the adornment of the church and the ritual of the liturgy? Was I somehow playing into the devil's hands even as I sought to get closer to heaven?

I MENTIONED MY UNEASE to my friend Joseph, way out in Wisconsin. He supported parish hopping. "Remember your Augustine. You're the bishop of your domestic church. Your family is your flock, and you have to be their shepherd. You have to do what's best for them." In other words, your children come first. When the priest says—and one did—that receiving communion wipes away your sins, no matter how big they are, church teaching is undermined. (Priest vs. church: How's *that* for a spirit of faction?) Daddy has to take the kids home and explain that receiving the Eucharist with serious sin on your soul is an offense against the sacrament, a sin in its own right. Shouldn't I offer them the best I can find, or at least a united front?

I thought of my own religious education. Before my confirmation in the faith, I was taught that sin was a breaking of the love relationship between God and me. That was true enough, but it didn't signify much to a fourteen-year-old with little to no sense of the importance of that "love relationship." I was never told about the possibility of mortal sin—sin that removes the soul from the life of grace, and opens up the real possibility of hell. I was never told that there were sins that required confession before communion could be worthily received. I heard too much in those CCD classes about love without obedience, heaven without hell, forgiveness without sin. And if I didn't understand sin, how could I understand redemption?

I thought of parish meetings, standing up and testifying about these educational failings in front of a bunch of religious ed teachers. I thought of my dad's failed attempt to fight the implementation of a particular sex education curriculum for the Syracuse diocese. The battle was thrust upon him—the psychology of the approach was inappropriate, so people came to the psychologist. The fight took no small amount of time and caused no small amount of stress at home, and the program ended up going in anyway. I shuddered at the thought of all that struggle. I didn't want parish life. I didn't want battles with liturgical committees and directors of religious education. I didn't want to write thoughtful letters. I just wanted to be left alone to raise my family in peace. But then, "go out and teach all nations . . ."

We stayed at Our Lady of the Sacred Heart for about five years. When Father Rich left to become a missionary, we left too. It turned out he had been what was holding us. Where to go? Mary and Ernie had never stopped attending Our Lady of the Rosary. We knew other families that attended. We headed back. The handshaking latecomers seemed to have stopped coming late. I didn't care much for the "ooo-ooo-ooos" that had made their way into the sung Our Father—". . . as we forgive those who trespass against us, ooo-ooo-ooo-ooo, and lead us not into temptation . . ." But I didn't let it upset me.

ᔌᔌᔌᔌᔌ

hand holding and other distractions

IT'S HARD to pay attention at Mass. When you're young, Mass can be deeply uninteresting. When you get older, you can become numb with familiarity. I have been attending Mass week in, week out for thirty-one years, and I am sure there are parts of the Eucharistic prayer I could not recite from memory. Advertising jingles from twenty years ago? No problem.

And no matter how interested I am in the proceedings, there are always distractions. An unruly child, possibly my own. My own worries and thoughts on other matters. My neighbor's hand, benevolently extended toward my own.

Hand holding during the Our Father is everywhere I go, it seems. I don't care much for it.

The practice may appear to some as a triumph of horizontal theology, of emphasizing the banquet part of the sacrificial banquet over the sacrificial part. But my chief objection, while similar, is more personal: It's distracting. At a time when I am supposed to be praying to God, I find myself thinking about the people next to me. I notice things like the feel of their hands—warm, cold, damp, dry, scaly, smooth—the firmness of their grip, how much they tremble or twitch. But even if these qualities didn't register, there would still be physical contact with another person.

I am attached to my senses. This is why I often close my eyes during prayer—to keep the sensible world from distracting me. But there is no closing the nerves in my hand. I cannot avoid the feeling of that hand that is not my own. I cannot help but be acutely aware of it, and God tends to take a backseat. I am joined in communion with my fellow man, but the whole point of our mutual endeavor—the worship of the Father—is lost. All that remains is the communion, and a shallow one at that, since I am holding hands not out of affection or fellowship, but because it is required of me.

I know we are saying the Our Father—emphasis on the "Our." I know Christ recommended communal worship when He said, "Where two or three are gathered in my name, there am I in the midst of them" (Matthew 18:20). But I wonder why we need this physical communion during the Our Father, when we are already joining our voices and our thoughts in common prayer to God. If people were to concentrate on the words they were saying in unison with their neighbor, wouldn't they sense a communion in their common praise and petition? "Give *us* this day our daily bread, and forgive *us* our trespasses, as we forgive those who trespass against *us*."

Now that hand holding has become standard practice, charity almost demands it. When that other hand extends toward me, it charges the air with expectation. It hangs in midair, creating an empty space where my hand ought to be. Not to fill that space would be an insult. I have heard stories of people who declined to hold hands being willfully ignored during the post–*Pater Noster* handshake of peace. The owner of the neglected hand was so offended he refused to offer it again as a sign of Christ's peace.

To avoid this rift, I submit to hand holding. I might resist on the grounds that I think it more important to do whatever is necessary to keep my focus on God, but the fact is, from the moment that hand is raised, my focus is blurred. Were my hands folded in front of me, I would be thinking about how the other person was feeling, whether they were offended, and if they were offended, how they were failing to judge me more charitably.

This would be an uncharitable judgment on *my* part—not only would I be distracted, I'd be sinning. I would resent the practice all the more, and also the person next to me who sought to practice the practice. Best to just hold hands, muddle through, and get used to it.

OTHER DISTRACTIONS ARE MORE SERIOUS, and tempt me toward more serious judgments. I have always had an unfortunate tendency to notice my fellow churchgoers, even when they aren't talking over the homily. *That's an awful lot of flesh she's showing. Spaghetti straps; tight shirt, short skirt—what is this, Our Lady of the Hotties? . . . Is that blank-eyed, shuffling punk even thinking about where he is, what he's doing? . . . People dress better than this to go to parties!*

My outrage is in some way legitimate. Our Lord on the altar deserves the outward sign of respect that formal dress affords, and the virtue of modesty exists, in part, to avoid creating such distractions. But all the while I am thinking these things, I am not looking at the crucified Christ hanging behind the altar, thanking him for the blessing of His Body and Blood. I am not begging God to overlook my own sins, so that the sacrament may bring me "not condemnation, but health." Instead, I am giving in to distraction, forgetting God even as I get ready to eat Him. I raise my eyes, bent on repentance, but they drop again to behold my imperfect neighbor. I am to blame, I know, but I feel like the devil is tugging at my retinas.

One Sunday at Our Lady of the Sacred Heart, as the opening hymn entered into its final verse, a group came in near the side entrance just in front of us. I always chose a place near the side entrance, so that I could leave unobtrusively if one of my children became too much of a distraction for others. But I had not yet learned that I should sit one or two rows in front of said entrance, so as not to be tempted to wonder about latecomers, even silent latecomers. *We're already to the Gospel. Don't these people care about offenses against the priest? The Mass? Our Lord?*

A harsh judgment, and what do you know, I carry this particular beam in my own eye. How many times have I humped it down the aisle with a baby in tow, well into the opening hymn or the confession of sins? And who knows what caused my neighbors' tardiness? Who knows their souls? Not me.

This particular group consisted of a boy—I'd put his age at around two—and two women, both of whom looked to be in their midforties. I was instantly struck by the impression that they were a homosexual couple, and that they had adopted this wan little redhead.

Though I accept the church's teaching that homosexual sex is fundamentally disordered, I do not experience moral horror in the face of homosexuals. It's not that I am necessarily more virtuous than people who *are* horrified; virtue would consist more in the soul's response to the horror. Nor do I have any kind of objection to a homosexual person being Catholic. All Catholics promise to reject sin when they renew their baptismal vows, and unless they proclaim otherwise, I have to assume that homosexual Catholics make the same promise. I have to assume that they seek to live chastely. I have to hope they understand that all sexual life is under God's authority; straight or gay, single or married—we are none of us the makers of its meaning.

I did not even know for certain that these women were gay. It was just a feeling, gathered from the way they looked at each other. I scolded myself for jumping to conclusions, and for even considering the matter during Mass. Charity demanded I think the best of them, whatever their sexual orientation. While I was at it, why was I thinking of them at all, when I should have been participating in the Mass? These women were not my business.

As if on cue, one woman reached over and began tracing circles with her hand on the other's back. I recognized in her touch the intimacy present in the way I touch my wife, whose body I know so well. *Ah-ha! So I was right!*

Of course, the touch was not really proof that I was right, and it did not change the fact that I ought not to be thinking ill of anyone, or about the matter at all. I did not know the road they walked. I did not know their relation to Christ. I was tempted by the thought that I was only curious and defensive for His sake, that I didn't want Him to be dishonored by an unrepentant sinner's reception of communion. If known adulterers tried to receive, they could rightly be denied communion, couldn't they? Was this similar?

Stop! You don't know! You receive with a host of sins on your soul, and probably more that you don't even know about. You don't know how they stand with God! You don't even know if they're homosexuals, if they're practicing homosexuals, if they even know the church's teaching! You don't know! Stop looking at them! Look at the priest! Look at the cross! Look at your own soul!

I wrestled the question and my reaction back down, steeling myself against the temptation to wonder. I tried not to look at the boy, even as he looked back at me, tried not to wonder about his growing up with "two mommies." I tried not to wonder about their reaction to Father's sermon on the Gospel, the one in which Christ says that "he who does not take his cross and follow me is not worthy of me," and that "he who loves father or mother more than me is not worthy of me" (Matthew 10:38, 37). I tried not to insert, "Or lesbian lover!" after "mother" in the verse. It was awful. If I was concerned, I should have said a prayer for them. I beg forgiveness.

ᴊᴏ ᴊᴏ ᴊᴏ ᴊᴏ ᴊᴏ

the world, . . .

FATHER LOUIS AT OUR LADY OF THE ROSARY was the first priest I ever heard invoke the great trinity of obstacles to sanctity: the world, the flesh, and the devil. I knew about struggles with the flesh, and even a thing or two about the devil. But I had grown up thinking that the goods of the world were God's blessings. Of course, you couldn't be covetous or attached, but surely there was no harm in enjoying what you came by honestly?

When Father Louis spoke of "the world," I did not take him to mean the earthly glories that Christ Himself warned against: power, prestige, wealth, luxury. I took him to mean creation in general. This was not because of anything Father Louis said; it was because of St. Augustine. In college, I had run up against Augustine's claim that the goods of the world were good only if their use disposed one to better love their creator. They were not to be enjoyed in themselves, for their own sake.

I had no rebuttal, but I couldn't quite give myself to the idea, even after my friend Karyn gave me a beautiful statue of St. Francis, standing with a skull at his feet.

"Why the skull?"

"To remember death. If you keep death before you, you won't get too caught up in the world."

So *that* was the temptation offered by the world—to distract us from death. My intellect nodded in apprehension; my will pretended not to notice. The goods of this world still look good to me, so good that I all but forget the spiritual aspect of life. So good that I think of life merely having a spiritual aspect, as opposed to thinking of the spiritual life as the preeminent life, the only one that matters in the end. "And over here, we have the spiritual life, useful on Sundays and in times of need . . ."

꒰꒱꒰꒱꒰꒱

BACK IN COLLEGE, I met a former student who was known for starting statements with, "Boy, if we weren't Catholic, we could . . ."—insert debauchery here. I presume he was at least half joking, but something about the notion offended me. Looking back from the vantage point of a few years, I think it was the idea that the faith was something entirely extrinsic, a set of rules we had to submit to, contrary to our heart's desires. That it did not entail an interior transformation, but merely a more perfect habit of external obedience.

I was offended because he had spoken what I kept silent in my own heart, and I was ashamed. I found—I find—that my own occasional wishes for forbidden pleasures spring from precisely this intellectual habit: regarding the faith as extrinsic, and being satisfied with obedience to the most extrinsic strictures it imposes.

There is a passage from Walker Percy's novel *The Moviegoer* that has stayed with me since the first time I read it. Protagonist Binx Bollings gives the following description of his uncle: "Uncle Jules is the only man I know whose victory in the world is total and unqualified. He has made a great deal of money, he has a great many friends, he was Rex of Mardi Gras, he gives freely of himself and his money. He is an exemplary Catholic, but it is hard to know why he takes the trouble. For the world he lives in, the City of Man, is so pleasant that the City of God must hold little in store for him. . . . No shadow ever crosses his face, except when someone raises the subject of last year's Tulane-LSU game" (Walter Percy, *The Moviegoer* [Franklin Center: the Franklin Library, 1980], 26). (The description made me wonder if Percy had read his Pagnol, so closely did it match my impression of Uncle Jules in *My Father's Glory*.)

I remember this passage because I recognize in it an image of the life I would like to have. Ah, to be rich and generous and popular and at ease with my place in the world—and a good churchman on top of it all. But I also remember the chill that comes from that suggestion, "the City of God must hold little in store for him." The words call up the unease I feel when I read in St. Paul, "My desire is to depart and be with Christ, for that is far better" (Philippians 1:23) and in John's Gospel, "He who loves his life loses it, and he who hates his life in this world will keep it for eternal life" (John 12:25).

I don't desire to depart. I don't hate my life. I like my life: my wife and children, my family and friends, my beautiful stuff. I like effort and accomplishment, the alternation of trials and triumphs. I like my connection to what's around me, the pleasure I take from good company, from eating and drinking well, from resting comfortably in my small world. And though I can tell myself it's silly to embrace these possessions too tightly, since all that I have has been given to me, I still cling to what I've got as if it's all there is.

What I've got is very, very good, far better than most of the world. But it would be a terrible mistake to let my relatively easy life get in the way of strengthening my connection to

God. I have taken to turning the water to cold at the end of my shower each morning and saying three Hail Marys as my flesh suffers, if only a little. I started the practice during Lent of 1998, as a simple mortification, but now I am attaching a further significance to it. I am hoping that this exterior tickle of discomfort will be a reminder that the world is not paradise, no matter how satisfied I feel. I am hoping that the shock of cold will rouse me from my God-forgetting material stupor, and remind me to offer Him, along with this brief suffering, my entire day.

I GET SOME HELP from Scripture in my endeavor to escape the world's warm embrace. In particular, there are two Gospel readings that, when I hear them read at Mass, break through the crust of familiarity and send a cold stab of fear into the heart of me. One is the parable of the wise and foolish maidens. The foolish, who bring no extra oil for their lamps, must go to the merchant when the bridegroom arrives late at night. Upon their return to the house, they find the door shut. When they cry, "Lord, Lord, open to us," they receive the devastating reply, "Truly, I say to you, I do not know you" (Matthew 25:1–12).

I think about God and the faith, and I hope my thinking has some spiritual worth. But knowing a great deal *about* God is not knowing *God.* Faith in Him is bound up with knowing

Him, and woe to me if my faith is borrowed from the true faith of others. Because if I do not know Him, I fear He will not know me, and the door will be shut.

Worse, I sometimes confuse thinking about the church with thinking about God. My father once gave me a subscription to *The Wanderer*, a Catholic newspaper that attracts adjectives like "ultraorthodox." He read it as a balance to the *National Catholic Register*, which, at the time, seemed to be full of good news and "all is well with the church." When *The Wanderer* was ringing forth its cries of "No Surprise" at the outset of the priestly abuse scandals, the *Register* seemed more interested in scolding the secular media for its handling of the issue. There is merit to both approaches, but *The Wanderer* gets to have more fun, as evidenced by headlines like, "Bishops in Usual Disarray: Liberals Advance Usual Agenda."

But where my father reads to stay informed, I read (at least in part) because I have a morbid taste for bad news, a fascination with the evil that men do. I read and shake my head in wonder. Indulging that morbid taste can feel awfully righteous. "Those monsters. How can they do those things?" And there I am, full of religious feeling and miles from anything approaching holiness. The church must dwell in the world; it must employ fallible human agents. If I let that worldly element become a distraction, then paying attention to the life of the church can become a barrier to charity. It certainly won't help me know Jesus.

THE OTHER GOSPEL READING stabs even deeper. It is the parable of the sower, in which the scattered seed stands for the word sown among different sorts of people. It scares me because I fear the loss of faith.

I don't fear that my faith will be like the seed that lands on rocky ground, springing up with joy but withering when tribulation comes. I sometimes joke with my friends that the reason my life is so easy is that God knows my faith is weak, and that any real test would send me skittering away from Him like a dry leaf in the wind. And it is certainly true that I have not suffered much. But while my faith may be weak, I'm not sure it's weak in that way. Just as I don't base my faith on a personal experience of God, I don't imagine that any particular personal suffering would make me doubt His existence, any more than it would make me doubt that water is wet. I do not tie up God's existence, or even His love, with the suffering of the world. My God is the God of Job. He is not indicted by the agonized "Why?" sent heavenward. When I read about the martyrs, I daydream about mirroring their heroism on Christ's behalf, and it does not seem beyond me. It seems like courage in battle, with the promise of Valhalla to those who do not falter.

The daydream that gets to me, the one that comes unbidden and unwelcome, involves a cushiony death at a ripe old age, or being hit by a car tomorrow—unheroic death, death without the clear connection to God that martyrdom provides. Those are the daydreams that end with me wondering—despite all my education and formation, all my blessings, all my years of churchgoing—if the grave is the end, if darkness and the void are waiting, if this life is all there is.

Religion, which bids us consider the life after this, makes so much more sense to me when it accounts for *this* life. When I think of heaven—let's not even start on hell—my confidence shivers. I have not lost my five-year-old's fear of eternity. I cannot rejoice in the thought of being happy forever in heaven, most likely because, while God is my God, He is not my friend. Or rather, I am not His. I have not developed the intimacy that would make me desire eternity in His company. "I do not know you." At these moments, I wonder if I have faith. I fear I am letting faith go untended, letting the world choke it out of me.

ᴏᴏᴏᴏᴏ

IF FAITH IS A GIFT, as Augustine says, then it is not deserved, but gratuitously given. If it is not deserved, then it may be taken away without offending justice. My God. What if I lose my faith? And do I really still have it? Sometimes, in the middle of the Creed, as I repeat the well-worn words about Light from Light and True God from True God, I find myself asking, "Do I really believe all that? What an extraordinary list of statements!"

I think my faith has a strong intellectual infrastructure, but bizarre events seem to draw me away from intellect. I cannot bear to think of the vastness of space. If humanity is a singular creation, so beloved by God that He redeemed it by the death of His Son, what is all that vastness doing there? I am shaken by images from the Hubble telescope; there are times when simply gazing into the night sky frightens me. Another time, I was upset by a TV special showing videos of supposed UFOs. Hard to see aliens' place in salvation history: If they have reason, they share in the image of God. Did they fall? Were they saved? How?

Goofy stuff; why am I so troubled? Suddenly I forget the historical fact of Jesus Christ; the marvelous integrity of the Catholic account of the world and man's place in it; the events in my own life that so clearly manifest God's love for me. I find myself grasping at childish reassurances. Every time I pray to St. Anthony, I find whatever I was looking for. Every time I say the St. Thérèse prayer and ask her to "pick a rose for me from the Heavenly Garden," I receive a rose of some kind. Thank heaven for the communion of saints, but these considerations ought to flow *from* faith, not give it substance.

Most often, I get out of these little crises by turning to love. Love seems to me the great reality that argues against religion being an intellectual construct—the manifest reality of the love affair between holy men and women and their God. You can't love empty air as these people love. I think of the saints, of certain priests I have known, of my own mother. I think of the times when I have been overwhelmed by love: that day in the Basilica of St. Francis during my Italian pilgrimage, when contemplating God as a Franciscan priest seemed so appealing. Once after receiving the Eucharist at Midnight Mass on Christmas.

The Eucharist, love incarnate, God in the world. Once, when my older brother was visiting, we were approached outside a movie theater by an evangelizing Protestant. These people make me go weak in the knees; I walked away, knowing my brother could handle himself and that these things are often best conducted one on one. Afterwards, he told me, "I used to get into it with them, going through Scripture and sort of making the case. Now, I just say, 'What does God want from us? Holiness. What is holiness? Union with God. How do we attain union with God? Through the Eucharist.' I cut right to it."

My brother is a theologian; doubtless, he can anticipate some objections to this line of argument. But there is something powerful—something essential—in it, and also something extremely attractive to me. Rather than stumbling over the idea of the Body, Blood, Soul, and Divinity appearing under the aspect of the Host, I *relish* the thought of eating God, achieving the most perfect union with Him I can while in this life. "He who eats my flesh and drinks my blood abides in me, and I in him" (John 6:56).

The fear that my faith can be explained away is forever working at me. Sometimes, I wonder if I'm just trying to lend drama to what otherwise would be a drab suburban life, loading up mundane realities with eternal significance. My belief in the devil? An attempt to place the locus of evil outside myself. My adherence to the church's teaching on sexual matters? Putting sex on a Procrustean bed, so as to hack off and ignore its messier, more complicated aspects. My belief in the afterlife? Simple fear of death. But when I receive communion, I am not suspicious of my joy. I do not fear that self-delusion. I am confident in the reality behind the appearance.

Attending Mass has always been my most fruitful spiritual exercise. There may be in this some vestige of a childish attitude that religion should occur at the proper time and place, instead of informing one's whole life. But there is more to it than that: The Mass is where I get the Eucharist.

Part of the attraction and that fruitfulness, no doubt, comes from my earthly temperament. I often find myself mired in the concrete, immediate particular. Until I achieve a more intimate relationship with Christ, this can make prayer difficult. Most often, I still experience prayer as missives to a far-off God who hears my words after they float up to heaven, instead of dialogue with a God nearer to me than I am to myself. But at Mass, bolstered by the anticipation or the memory of communion, I do better. I am better disposed to turn my attention from the physical world toward the spiritual, since the spiritual has become physical. God is physically within me, and that makes it easier to talk to Him.

I feel more familiar with Him as I kneel and recite the ALTAR Prayer, which my mother learned from her own mother and taught me before my first communion, years ago: "Lord, I *Adore* you for . . . I *Love* you for . . . I *Thank* you for . . . I *Ask* you for . . . I *Resolve* to . . ." Simple as it is, it has not lost its savor. I should get to Mass more often. I should pray more. Prayer is the way out of the world, and prayer is where I fail. I cringe at my friends' casual mentions of family rosaries—why don't I do that? I don't have twenty minutes a day?

ᴓᴓᴓᴓᴓ

MY FRIEND MARY is one of those family rosary people, a big believer in formal prayer. Like me, she hails from the Irish-molded east. She advocates Morning Offerings to cover the joys and sorrows of the day to come:

> O Jesus, through the Immaculate Heart of Mary,
> I offer You all my prayers, works, joys, and sufferings of
>   this day,
> for all the intentions of Your Sacred Heart,
> in union with the Holy Sacrifice of the Mass through-
>   out the world,
> in reparation for my sins, for the intentions of all our
>   associates,
> and in particular for the intentions of the Holy Father.

Her husband, Ernie—California-born and less shaped by a particular ethnic rendering of the faith—argues for a less structured prayer life, something more in line with Paul's exhortation to pray constantly. A given day provides endless opportunities for petition, thanksgiving, repentance, and the offering up of suffering. Life, he says, can interfere with formal devotions, but that needn't leave you feeling like you've neglected our Lord and our Lady.

Their back-and-forth is friendly enough, and they both know that one side doesn't work to the exclusion of the other. A Morning Offering will not automatically correct a will that is struggling to accept some suffering—the act must be made in the moment. And the testimonies of countless saints—not to mention the explicit request from the Virgin Mary that we pray the rosary—indicate the necessity and benefit of time devoted formally to prayer. My father again, this time quoting St. John Vianney: "At the beginning of the day, God has the necessary grace for the day ready for us. He knows exactly what opportunities we shall have to sin, and will give us everything we need if we ask Him then. That is why the devil does all he can to prevent us from saying our morning prayers or to make us say them badly" (Saint Jean-Marie-Baptiste Vianney, *Thoughts of the Curé D'Ars* [Rockford, IL: Tan Books and Publishers, Inc., 1984], 18).

As for me, I'm getting better at starting the day with the readings from *Magnificat*. But all too often, my prayer has the character of sacrifice, giving God time at the start of the day, before turning to my own concerns. There's merit to that; at the very least, I find that I'm better able to deal with temptation during the rest of the day. But it's a long way from lifting up my heart to the Lord, coming to know Him, becoming His friend. Too often, I feel that my prayers are borrowed things, unless they are simple petitions. There is no conversation. I do not hear; I probably don't even really listen. More is needed.

ᕫᕫᕫᕫᕫ

. . . the flesh, and the devil

WHILE VISITING JERRY, a guy I know, I happened upon a magazine entitled *Submissive Girls.* The photo on the back cover showed a woman, standing, bound and gagged, her naked breasts cinched by straps. She stared out at me with eyes full of rage. This surprised me; I imagined helpless fear would be the desired expression. But then, bondage porn was new to me. I knew all about lust. I knew how it reduced a woman from person to tool. I knew because I had done it myself often enough. This time, however, I was not titillated. It was not my thing.

The trouble was, it was Jerry's thing. I had heard about his stash, but had never said anything. Imagine:

"Hey Jerry, I hear you've got a bunch of porn."

"Yeah, Matt, what about it? It's okay to work up an appetite, as long as I eat dinner at home, right?" (Jerry is married.)

"Well, Jerry, Jesus said that if a man looks at a woman with lust in his heart, he has already committed adultery with her."

Oh, Lord, no. It would be hard enough to bring up if we were of like minds about the matter. But though he was Catholic, I knew Jerry didn't think lust was a problem. Jerry thought sexual purity was women's talk. Us boys had our own understanding.

He was not alone in this opinion. I was once told in the confessional that viewing a certain amount of pornography was normal and natural. If it got to be excessive . . . well, then I should seek counseling. By "normal and natural," I don't think the priest meant that many men have a weakness for it, and that I shouldn't add self-loathing to my troubles. I think he meant that since many men have a weakness for it, it wasn't that big a deal. I wasn't about to argue with him from behind the screen, but I knew better. I knew that the *Catechism* condemned pornography as a grave offense, since it removed sex from its proper context. And even without the *Catechism*, I knew in my bones.

But whatever I knew and however I knew it, wasn't there some part of me that agreed with Jerry? Wasn't there something in my soul that associated sexual purity with stultified prig-gishness, instead of a manly struggle for the virtue of chastity? When I made a conscious effort to take the old-fashioned advice and "keep custody of the eyes"—even going so far as to look the other way when passing the fleshy spreads in the windows of Victoria's Secret at the mall—didn't I hear a little voice saying I was going too far? "It's not that big a deal. By straining to avoid it, you make it a greater temptation than it really is."

But however big or small a deal, it remained an offense. And now, here was Jerry's offense, right in front of me. In his book *Mere Christianity*, C. S. Lewis wrote of human nature that "the rats are always there in the cellar." Fallen nature is never entirely eradicated; it's always down there in the dark. Finding that magazine, I felt like I had caught a rat unawares as it ventured into the kitchen—Jerry's rat. If the rat hated me for catching him, I hated him more for letting himself get caught, for not staying in the basement so I could ignore him and go about my business. As it was, I felt that I had to do something. I hadn't been snooping when I found *Submissive Girls*. I felt that my finding it was a call, one I desperately didn't want to hear.

A big part of my trouble was pride. I knew he would think I was a fool—or at least, I thought I knew. I knew he would think I was unsophisticated, or uptight, or maybe just whipped.

"The wife's got a pretty tight grip on you, doesn't she, Matt?"

"This has got nothing to do with her."

"Mm-hm."

In my weakness, I wished that priests would talk about lust more, that I had the pulpit to back me up. But that didn't matter now.

I wrote him a letter, longhand. I must have gone through six drafts, trying to get the tone right. I wanted him to know that I didn't think myself holier-than-thou, that I regarded myself as a fellow sinner. I wanted him to know that I was writing out of love. I did call on authority by quoting the *Catechism*, but I included personal testimony as well. I wrote about how lust can drive a wedge between spouses, including lust after a stranger in a photograph. I shared the prayers I say when tempted, told him about the pardon and strength that come from confession. I left the letter by the door to his basement workshop, where I figured his wife wouldn't find it.

I don't know if he read the letter. He never responded, and I haven't asked him about it, though we see each other every year or so. I sometimes wonder if he's forgotten about it, just as I so often forget about it. I rarely pray for him, though I know I should. I still feel foolish, still stumble in my attempt to witness.

One thing I didn't write about was my practice of saying three Hail Marys under cold water at the end of my shower. I figured that if Jerry thought worrying about lust was uptight and old-fashioned, then the notion of mortifying the flesh was positively medieval. (Those poor three Hail Marys—how much I lay upon them!) I did not tell Jerry how I silently proclaim, in the hopes of its one day being true, "Lord, I love you more than my life" as I wait for the water to make its shocking shift from hot to cold.

I do that every day except Sundays and Holy Days. But I sometimes slack off when I'm sick, and I'm not always in a hurry to resume once I return to health. So when I got back under the icy streams following an Easter tinged with frustration and the flu, and added to my efforts a renewed effort at daily prayer, the enemy apparently took note. Right alongside my increase in spiritual exercise came an increase in Satan's interest in me.

ℛℛℛℛℛ

HE TENDS TO LEAVE ME ALONE when I'm not struggling to escape his dominion—and I do believe in his dominion. Christ called him the prince of this world. But a recent meditation from *Magnificat* included this from St. Augustine: "At the time when it was said to the devil, 'You shall eat earth,' it was said to the sinner, 'You are earth, and into earth shall you go.' What is here implied is that the sinner has been handed over as food for the devil." He doesn't like it when his dinner makes a break for it.

I gauged Satan's increased interest in part by a sharp increase in temptations toward my more familiar sins—lust, impatience, and sloth. Also anxiety. I constantly worried over this and that, failing to trust in God. And I found myself breaking new ground, digging new cesspools in my interior landscape. I started speaking unkind words, harboring ill will, giving in to detraction and harsh judgment. Anger, which had not yet revealed the full measure of its presence in my temperament, started to bubble up and boil over.

The only benefit from all this was the assurance that I was doing something right. God can manage just fine without the devil. Lucifer was once an angel, after all. But if there's a devil, then there must be a God. And if the devil was trying to trip me up, I must actually have been going somewhere.

I ONCE MET AN OLD MONSIGNOR who complained that people were far too quick to look for the devil's hand in evils of the world. He said that the evil in the heart of man was sufficient to account for a great many crimes. From what little I know of my own heart, he was certainly right about its wretched sufficiency for evildoing. But that doesn't mean the devil isn't real. The Gospels testify to his existence, as does the church. When we are invited to renew the vows of our baptism, the series of questions still opens with, "Do you reject Satan? And all his works? And all his empty promises?" (I like to imitate my father in my response, booming my enthusiastic "Yes!" as if the sheer volume of it could drive Lucifer further away.)

The devil is a part of the faith I have accepted. I do not feel driven to confirm his existence from experience. If I did, I think I would have an easier time than if I were hunting for God. Personally, as in my experience of the Eucharist, there are times when I am simply confident in the presence of a supernatural force. Perhaps a skeptic could explain my dream of a child with a twisting, melting face and a poisoned blade between his teeth, biting my hand and setting my blood on fire. Perhaps he could explain my memory—however fuzzy—of hearing the voices of hell broadcast over my dorm-room stereo in the middle of the night, inviting me to join them. Perhaps he could explain the malice that sometimes supervenes in my soul during fights with my wife. I am willing to accept psychological explanations for many things. In these instances, I am convinced otherwise.

My family has always taken the devil seriously, in particular, as a sower of discord. Once a year, our whole family gathers together, and it should be a joyous occasion. There are no deep rifts among us, no long-simmering grudges. But then, soon after that first happy exchange of greetings, he comes. Just the wrong thing said at just the wrong time, sore spots touched, emotions snowballing until charity is tossed by the wayside and people are thinking only of their personal wounds. In a family like mine, where theology is often discussed, this must bring the devil special pleasure. Sinning over God-talk—fabulous.

It is not always enough for one of us to pull back and name names, to say, "This is an attack from the devil." But it certainly helps. If we said the old St. Michael's prayer a little more often, I imagine that would help as well.

St. Michael the Archangel, defend us in battle; be our protection against the wickedness and snares of the devil. May God rebuke him, we humbly pray. And do thou, O prince of the heavenly host, by the power of God, cast into hell Satan and all the evil spirits who prowl about the world seeking the ruin of souls.

I love that prayer. I like the words associated with demonic action: *snares, prowl, ruin*. The devil is a tricky fellow.

Hanging in my office is a print of an etching made by Jacques Callot of *The Temptation of St. Anthony*. It's a poor man's version of the famous Bosch painting; the demons are more ridiculously ugly than truly horrifying, though they do cavort in Bosch-like manner, especially with regard to sticking things in each other's bottoms. What I like about Callot's version is that Satan puts in a grand personal appearance, filling the sky along the top of the picture. His dragon-head is turned, not toward the tiny image of the saint in the bottom right-hand corner, but toward the viewer. His eyes gaze balefully outward: "Here's looking at you, kid."

I like to be able to see him. On the actual battlefield of my interior, he can be difficult to spot, hiding as he does amid the World and the Flesh. From the aforementioned Augustine passage: "By overcoming within ourselves the inordinate love for things temporal, we are necessarily, within ourselves, overcoming him also who rules within man by these sinful desires."

I know I have to be careful with the devil. I don't want to shunt off my personal failings onto him—my evil is my own. Satan won't be around at the judgment to share the blame. But I don't want to discount his power and influence, either. To ignore him is to let him move unseen, which is exactly where he thrives. I don't want to be cocky with him. I sympathize with the old tradition of not saying his name, for fear of giving him an inroad. But neither do I want to cower before him. I believe I have power over him; the thing is not to suppose that the power is my own.

ᴊᴏᴊᴏᴊᴏᴊᴏᴊᴏ

dredging my soul for sin

THE WORLD, THE FLESH, AND THE DEVIL work on my will, but my will, bent and feeble as it is, would have trouble enough without them. I have heard that St. Pio of Pietrelcina was such a tremendous confessor that he would tell people their sins when they came to him. How thrilling; how terrifying.

Thrilling because here is a man who truly sees with the eyes of God, who acts *in persona Christi* in an explicit fashion. It's a little like the Eucharistic miracle at Lanciano, Italy. The story is that, at a Mass in the church of St. Legonthian some twelve hundred years ago, the bread and wine offered in the consecration—by a priest plagued by doubts about the real presence—were transformed into actual heart tissue and blood. (The flesh and blood remain there to this day, encased in glass.) In both cases, the mysterious aspect of the sacrament is removed; you are made to know what you are eating, and what you are doing in the confessional box. You are confessing your sins not to a mere man—though a man hears your sins, gives counsel, and speaks the words of absolution—but to a man taking the part of Christ.

Terrifying because here is a man who will tell you your sins—not the ones you have bundled up and brought as an offering, but the ones you hold back, hopefully through ignorance and tepid inquiry. I think again of the miracle at Lanciano; the veil torn away from the fact of the sacrifice, the fact of blood—blood that ought to be ours—being shed. A painful and wonderful sight. In the box with a man like St. Pio, you confess the sins that weigh on your conscience, and that is good. But then he takes you further. He uncovers the infestations that have taken such hold that they feel a part of you, the ones you cannot imagine excising.

૭ા૭ા૭ા૭ા૭ા

MY OWN LIST OF SINS is forever ready at hand; I can't remember my last really searching examination of conscience. I know I should search harder. I know that the deeper I dig, the more muck I dredge up and bring before Christ in confession, the more I may obtain His mercy. This should make me rejoice. How blessed I am; Christ wants to forgive me my very worst offenses. I should think it wonderful to be able to show Him those blackest stains and have Him not recoil in horror but lovingly wipe them away. The more sins I confess, the more sins He forgives, the more I will be able to live in "the glorious liberty of the children of God" (Romans 8:21). The effort ought to be exhilarating, and if I ever get spiritually fit, I imagine it will be so.

I try to think of a convert, someone who has just discovered the possibility of God's mercy. How happy he must be to finally unload all that weighty baggage. He would understand Father Steckler's "Excellent, excellent" as the sins came tumbling forth. Father is rejoicing to see a soul, hardened and encrusted by years of neglect and violence, finally made pristine—every surface scrubbed, every crevice scraped. The convert is rejoicing as well. The shame of all that sin, however great, is eclipsed by gratitude for the great goodness of God. "Yes, isn't it excellent? All these awful transgressions; I present them to Jesus, and he removes them all!"

I lack that zeal. What I have is some of that silly pride, which wants to put on its best face for God. "Doing my best here; if you could just give me a hand with these few things. Thanks so much." What I should do is lay open every secret, festering sore and beg for healing.

THROUGH SOME UNLOOKED-FOR GRACE, I have of late come to recognize two sins, both of them ingrained in my temperament and sealed by habitual practice. The first was difficult to spot;

its commission did not excite attention until I saw its effect on my wife. The first sin was constant wanting.

I want endlessly and am full of anxiety because of it. The house—yet another, with more land, thanks to the upward spiral of the real-estate market—provides a fine starting list. After that, there are books, music, travels—*time*. When one desire is fulfilled or passes or, oh so rarely, is defeated, another is never long in taking its place. My heart is restless indeed. *What's next?* And because I am full of want, I am empty of gratitude. My offense is twofold: against my wife, who loves me so well and is pricked by my apparent dissatisfaction with the life we share; and against God, who has given me the many blessings I ignore. Fighting it will require cultivating a habit of gratitude. Thanking God continually. Practicing self-denial. Mortify, mortify. That's the least I can do; at best, I hope to find rest in friendship with God. When Mom says, "Whatever God wants," she knows whereof she speaks.

The second sin was much more conspicuous, once it made its grand appearance. For a while, it showed up as peevishness, irritation, impatience. It showed up when I attempted to fast, or when I was tired, or stressed. I chalked it up to circumstance. But now I know it for what it is: plain old anger, one of the seven deadlies. A sin I never really understood in other people, because I had never really felt its full power. Then I got married. Then I had kids.

Temper runs in my family. I have known this, at some level, ever since my brother and I witnessed my grandfather's intense irritation at a waitress's failure to bring him really boiling hot water for his tea. His entire body looked angry. Later, I watched with admiration as my father battled his father's curse. I saw how prayer can help a man overcome sin, even sin that's in the blood.

But now it was my turn, and I seemed to be the worst of the bunch. After seven years of marriage, I started exploding: the hand slammed down; the voice, out of control, ripping up out of the throat. Once or twice, I threw things—soft children's toys, not crockery, but still. Every time, the object was my wife or my children. And even if I could imagine offenses that warranted such reactions, I knew neither wife nor children had committed anything close to them.

The development left me shaken. With other sins, even other serious sins, it was different. There was still the tendency to look back in wonder—*What was I thinking? How could I do that?* But intellectually, I could still recognize myself in those sins. I knew what I was thinking. I knew how I did that, however unbelievable it appeared in retrospect. I recognized my fault; I knew where my sin came from.

It was different with anger. My rage scared me. My son choked his brother while they were wrestling. I bellowed and grabbed him by the shoulders. I stuck my face in his and growled.

"You choked your brother?"

"Yes," he whimpered.

I placed my hand on his throat. "Do you want me to choke you?"

"No!"

"WHY NOT?"

"Because then I can't breathe!"

"RIGHT! SO DON'T DO IT TO YOUR BROTHER!"

Another time, I pinned my son to the ground while I shouted at him. I didn't hurt him, but I could tell he was scared. I apologized for these outbreaks, told my children I was working on my anger, that I needed God's help just like they did. They forgave me. But it couldn't be like this. I was mystified and horrified by my behavior. I had no idea where it came from, and what was more, I did not recognize myself in the memory of my actions.

IT DIDN'T COME FROM MY FATHER, or my own upbringing. Dad got angry, but he never used that kind of physical intimidation.

And he wasn't mean. Once, I said to Fin, "Spare me the attitude—brat!" That was not like me. I didn't call people names, even people I strongly disliked. My father taught me to be better than that, and his lessons stuck. Even if someone performed a bratty action, even if they performed bratty actions habitually, you didn't identify the person with the fault. I didn't do that to anybody, except, apparently, my son.

Even if it didn't feel like me exploding, however—even if it was passion taking over—it was still me indulging that passion. It was still my will that surrendered to it so easily. I could chalk it up to a growing family, to stress about work, to financial strain, to frustration with my own failings, but it was still me behaving in intolerable ways, ways I never dreamed I would.

Passion is a tricky enemy. Avoiding the occasion is essential, of course, but even if you manage that, it still operates, often subrationally. And when you have kids, you can't really avoid the occasion for anger. It'll be there, usually every day. You have to overcome the tendency to indulge passion. I started by attacking it subrationally—through physical suffering, especially fasting. That helped a lot; my passions were pretty much quelled. It also left me weak, listless, and unmotivated at work. I stopped fasting. The explosions subsided;

I'm not entirely sure why. But I know it's in me. The rats are always in the cellar.

ৣৣৣৣৣ

the moviegoer
(plus a trip to the theater)

THERE'S A WONDERFUL LINE from Whit Stillman's film *Metropolitan*: Young Tom Townsend tells Jane Austen-loving Audrey, "I don't read novels. I prefer good literary criticism. That way, you get both the novelist's ideas as well as the critic's thinking." The aesthetic barbarity of the notion is hilarious, but even as I laugh, I shiver with recognition. How many times have I read the reviews of a book or film and left it at that?

Barbaric as my approach may be, it occasionally bears fruit. I am glad that I never saw *40 Days and 40 Nights*, but Charles Taylor's review of the film in the online magazine *Salon* provided its own measure of interest. At first, the movie had me curious. The story follows a guy's attempt to remain completely sex free—including masturbation—for forty days. In college, guys used to joke about giving up sex for Lent. Some sacrifice—giving up a sin you never committed anyway. But a film about a stud who tries to resist sexual temptation? How novel, how chock-full of comedic potential.

Upon reflection, however, I decided the thing couldn't fly. The will—the motive—counts for a great deal in these matters. Matt, the hero, doesn't give up sex because he believes it to be wrong, or because he thinks any good will come from it. He gives it up on a bet, to show that he can—pride taking the place of lust. Whatever insight he gained during his dry spell would be in the end an accidental good; the point was to grit your teeth and get through it. And when the forty days are over, *Let's get it on* . . .

Taylor's *Salon* review dismissed the film, but he did take the occasion to sound off on some of its themes. Taylor has written both defenses and appreciations of porn, so the tone of his comments wasn't a surprise. Still, it was interesting to note the particulars.

Taylor complained about the celibate preaching to the non-celibate. Matt's brother is a seminarian, from whom Matt seeks counsel about living the sex-free life. Taylor's jab: "Would you want advice about your sex life from someone who's not getting any?" Well, yes. Passion has a way of coloring perception. There's a reason masturbation was reputed to cause blindness—not physical, but spiritual. The hero is not seeking advice about sexual technique, he's trying to master his desires. It seems fair to hope for a clearheaded view from a nonparticipant, in particular, a nonparticipant who has had to battle his own temptations.

Taylor probably wouldn't grant the point. He wrote, "The trouble is, as the movie portrays it, Matt's enlightenment derives from his giving up sex—not from his being able to tell the difference between sex for fun and sex with a connection." He offered his own prescription, suggesting that "sleeping with lots of girls [is] one of the sanest and healthiest things you can do to get over a bad breakup." I imagine Taylor thinks that it helps to remind a person that sex needn't be a communion with your (former) beloved, it can just be a good time. As Ben said to Clara in *The Long, Hot Summer*: "I please you, you please me."

Is that appealing on some level? Yes. Does it make a measure of sense? Sure. Sex is fun. It's not as if Deirdre and I kneel by the bed to pray and reflect on the impending expression of our sacramental bond. But I'm claiming that sex has a deeper meaning even when I don't think about that meaning, even when I'm not seeking "sex with a connection." I'm claiming that there is a created order, independent of my will, and that sex within the context of my marriage conforms to that order in a way that a one-night stand does not.

What really amazed me, though, was Taylor's next paragraph: "Forget the implicit message that spirituality can't survive pleasure. The notion of giving things up—whether food or sex or shopping—for spiritual reasons is pretty narcissistic. Isn't sacrifice, in the Lenten sense, mostly just a way of showing your superiority to earthly matters? And never mind that a spirituality strengthened by giving up hamburgers or masturbation or a glass of wine with dinner seems only thimble-deep in the first place" (Charles Taylor, review of *40 Days and 40 Nights*, directed by Michael Lehmann, *Salon.com*, 1 March 2002).

Wow. I was used to seeing Catholics trashed for their views on morality, but mortification? My first response to Taylor's line about "thimble-deep spirituality" was that he must never have tried to give up anything he enjoyed—really *enjoyed*. A glass of wine with dinner (or two or three) is a great joy to me. It gladdens my heart. When I give it up for Lent, I miss it a lot. My second response to his claim was, "Maybe he *has* given these things up, and it hasn't proved difficult, because he had no religious intent. The devil, the tempter, would pay no attention to such a man—what would be the point?"

Finally, I balked at Taylor's use of "strengthened spirituality." I don't give things up for anything as abstract as strengthened spirituality. I give them up to please another person: God. When I fast, I hope to draw nearer to Him by detaching myself from the world. I don't think much about spirituality. Sacrificing earthly goods for Lent is a way of showing devotion to Him, not superiority to the world. That's not narcissism. That's love.

ღღღღღ

I DID SEE El Crimen del Padre Amaro (The Crime of Father Amaro), and I'm glad I did, if only for the help it gave me in sorting out the buzz surrounding the film. When it arrived from Mexico, virtually every two-bit review took a moment to note that it had broken box-office records south of the border. Those same reviews mentioned that it had sparked a controversy in Mexico, because, they said, it was about a young priest who takes up an affair with a sixteen-year-old girl. News stories about the controversy mentioned the two scenes that had come under the heaviest attack: one in which the young priest dresses up his paramour in a robe intended for a statue of Mary, and one in which an old woman feeds the consecrated Host to her cat.

The outrage over these scenes missed the mark; they were not the real trouble with *El Crimen del Padre Amaro*. Nor was the priestly dalliance. What a film shows and what it says are different things. It is tiresome to chant, "Context is all (or very nearly all)," but it's no less true for being tiresome.

A person might object to the fairly explicit sex scene between priest and schoolgirl. For many, it is at least the near occasion of sin to view on-screen nudity and intercourse. But that objection would stand regardless of whether or not one of the participants was a priest. And besides, there was no nudity or intercourse in the infamous Marian-robe scene. The line that got printed in the accounts of the controversy said that the film was "making fun of sacred symbols of our Faith," namely, the Virgin and the Host.

Come, now. See who is doing the robing, who is saying that his lover is "more beautiful than the Virgin": a priest with no real piety or morality. A priest who is willing to lie to further his career, who is willing to have sex with a young girl but not to leave his comfortable priestly life and marry her. A priest who suggests she have an abortion so that he will not be found out.

The only time we see Father Amaro at prayer is when he wants to be rescued from the earthly consequences of his sin. Those earthly consequences are clearly all that matter to him; he has already rejected an opportunity for confession. He is not simply a weak priest (like the pastor), nor is he a rebel priest who disobeys on principle (like the priest in the hill country). He is merely an empty priest, with no real faith or charity. The film has made his wretchedness clear; why is it outrageous when a wretched man does a wretched deed? How does it make fun of the Virgin? It reflects badly on the lust-addled Father, not Mary.

A more general objection might be that it is impious even to depict such a priest, an offense to the priestly office. But given the recent depiction of some priests being offered by real life, it's hard to feel the sting.

As for the other reportedly controversial scene: yes, it is outrageous that the Host should be fed to an animal. But see who is doing the feeding: a superstitious madwoman with no real piety or morality. A woman who views the wafer as "medicine" fit for either a cat or a developmentally disabled girl. Just stuff it in and watch the magic. How is the Host mocked when evil people are shown abusing it? Of course bad folks mistreat our Lord—nothing outrageous in that.

After seeing the film, I found myself doubting that the "controversial" scenes are what Mexican Archbishop Alberto Suárez Inda of Morelia had in mind when he said that the film was "loaded with hatred of our church." I suspect he was referring more to what the film was truly about. Father Amaro is not simply a priest who has an affair. He is a priest who, in the pursuit of his precious ecclesial career, commits crime after crime, eventually grinding a relatively innocent girl under the wheels of his ambition. He is aided and abetted in some of these crimes by his bishop. His fellow priests are either corrupt or spineless;

the one priest with integrity ends up excommunicated, and the one priest who repents ends up leaving the church.

The hatred I sensed, the hatred the archbishop saw, was expressed in the implication that God and faith have nothing to do with the institutional church, and that those Catholics who do have faith are pious dupes. The film depicts one diocese, but the thoroughness of the decay suggests something more universal: if you want to find a good man, don't go looking in the church.

ᵖₒᵖₒᵖₒᵖₒ

I TRIED TO AVERT MY EYES when Father Amaro undressed his girlfriend and joined her in making the beast with two backs. I was pretty successful, but I hated doing it. It feels awkward to look away. Part of the awkwardness is because the eye does not want to abandon the sight of attractive flesh. But part of it is more abstractly aesthetic. By looking away, I'm removing myself from the story, pulling myself back into the mundane world and its sensible talk of the near occasion of sin.

It's something of a no-win situation. One of the great problems of on-screen nudity (particularly female nudity) is its power to remove the viewer (particularly the male viewer) from the story being told, to narrow his vision and understanding to the point where it's just him and a naked woman. Susan Sarandon once said that a woman in a nude scene has a hard time not being upstaged by her nipples. One hears directors and actors talk of nudity being "necessary to the story," when in many cases, it is necessary to *avoid* nudity if the story is to be preserved in the viewer's mind. Whether I look or not, the story suffers.

Julianne Moore, who starred with Ralph Fiennes in the 1999 film adaptation of Graham Greene's novel *The End of the Affair*, appeared naked in several rather intense sex scenes. She is a fine actress, and I think she avoided being upstaged by her nipples. I found myself drawn to think more about her effect on Fiennes and his effect on her than about her effect on me. But she still made me arch and twist in my seat, as if seeking to flee the tableau on-screen. She still knocked me out of the story and into my own discomfiture. And in her first encounter with Fiennes, she did it without even taking her clothes off.

Though Moore remained dressed—Fiennes, overcome with desire, simply hiked up her skirt—the scene was explicit. The motions of intercourse were more clearly visible and more lengthily lingered over than elsewhere. And early on, there was a tremendously affecting shot of Fiennes's hand finding its way inside Moore's skirt and inside Moore herself. (I find myself thinking of Moore and Fiennes instead of the characters they played—there I am, knocked out of the story, a story I thought was great.)

By "affecting," I do not mean arousing. I was, paradoxically, too involved to be aroused. I mean that it produced a sympathetic twinge in me, a response to his desire and her pleasure, the violence of their emotions. But sympathy is not empathy; I didn't share their feelings. I was embarrassed.

The lovers were utterly exposed, completely unself-conscious in the midst of ecstasy. Moore's transported expression was almost painful to behold. It felt wrong to be an uninvolved witness to such passion. I felt the way I do when I want to politely turn away from someone overcome with grief. The person's interior life is exposed, with or without the consent of their will. To look would be invasive. (Porn, by way of contrast, is all nudity and no passion. As a result, it may be arousing, but it's not embarrassing. The embarrassment comes later.)

When it comes to creating intimacy, exposed grief doesn't even come close to exposed sexual ecstasy. In college, we often joked about "knowing someone in the biblical sense," a reference to the Old Testament's use of, ". . . went in and knew his wife." Calling carnal union a kind of knowing dovetailed nicely with the definition of knowledge commonly used at school—the union of the intellect with the form of a thing. Moore's character hinted at this when she talked about God's perfect knowledge of her; she said, "He knew me the way [my lover's] hands knew me." In *Lancelot*,

Walker Percy made it more explicit: "The Jews called it knowing and now I knew why," says Lancelot Lamar. "Every time I went deeper I knew her better. Soon I would know her secret" (Walker Percy, *Lancelot* [New York: Farrar, Straus & Giroux, 1977], 236).

Ecstasy reveals that secret. Watching Moore up on screen, watching that hand disappear into her skirt, I saw her secret revealed. But instead of drawing me in, instead of creating intimacy, the revelation drove me away. I knew her better than I should. It was too much.

ʂʊʂʊʂʊ

IF THE END OF THE AFFAIR imparted too much knowledge, the play *Damien* left me longing for more. The one-man show tells the true story of Damien de Veuster, a priest who devoted himself to caring for the denizens of the leper colony on the Hawaiian island of Molokai. (Damien eventually fell victim to leprosy himself.) I saw a local production put on by the Lamb's Players Theater. I think the production was good, and that the actor Robert Smyth gave a sound, sensitive portrayal of this heroic priest. And yet, I was strangely unmoved.

After the show, Smyth held an informal forum with the audience. During the forum, he said, "I love the fact that Damien is a flesh-and-blood human being. A lot of times, when we think of people who are saintly, it's kind of like [they have] this distance from us. [We have] kind of this little fuzzy image of, 'They're so special.' I like the fact that this is a very human portrayal of someone. At the same time, he has an immense compassion, and a very deep faith."

"Very human" here means, I think, fallible. Father Damien has a temper, and he seems to lose it most often in the presence of the board of health, which neglects the lepers it has promised to care for, and which makes his life difficult at every turn. He is tempted by the healthy, lusty daughter of a family he visits. He expresses fears that the praise afforded him in the press will breed pride in his soul. He battles with his bishop. And at the end, in what was for me the play's most dramatic moment, he gives full voice to his doubts.

The moment works because it digs into Damien's interior life, where the most important battles are fought, and which a one-man show may display to great effect. For the most part, the play is content to remain on the surface, telling the story of a holy man who not only laid down his life, but who effected change while alive. A good story, an inspiring story, but one that could have stood a few more self-probing soliloquies.

Damien gets angry at the board of health, but does anyone in the audience blame him? They come across as soulless bureaucrats. More interesting was Damien's confession of beating a leper he catches molesting a young boy, then threatening him with dire consequences if he ever catches him again. Here, Christ could have risen to the surface. Imagine Damien remembering that Christ came to call sinners, sinners like that child molester. Damien is trying to bring Christ's love to these people, and here he has lost his temper and inflicted violence on the sort of person he should be trying hardest to save. Imagine Damien realizing that Christ wants him to apologize to the molester for his wrathful actions, to humble himself so that the molester's heart might be turned to Christ. But the play stops with the confession.

Damien has to overcome his revulsion at the physical wretchedness of the lepers, but we never hear a word about his reaction to their spiritual wretchedness, their soul-twisting battles with bitterness and despair—which surely must have taken place, and with which he must have been involved. The bishop, who objects to Damien's administering the sacrament of last rites to non-Catholics, is almost of necessity seen as the enemy. Damien is the missionary of love to these poor souls, and this bishop is obsessing over distinctions. But shouldn't Damien, who has a great love for the sacraments—especially confession—have at least paused over the bishop's objection? And the fear of pride, a worthwhile theme, is introduced, but then left alone until the moment of doubt at the end.

Damien asks God if the accusations that have been leveled against him are true, if he did more harm than good and followed not God but his own temperament. He asks for a word of reassurance, and there is a moment of tension as he waits, and waits, and finally speaks into the silence that if his doubts are what come between him and his Lord, then he will cast them aside. "You are my God," he concludes, "and I am Your priest." He smiles with the joy of this statement, and his face is lit with radiant light.

THINKING ABOUT THE PLAY, I found myself thinking about another play, one as yet unwritten. It's about a priest who gives himself to preaching in front of abortion clinics. Like the poor Father in *Diary of a Country Priest*, everything he does will seem to him a failure. Everything will make him feel he's the wrong man for the job. He will be stunned into silence by the wrath of pro-choicers who accuse him of hating women and sex, unable to even begin to explain himself. The pro-life faithful will be angry with him because he seems more interested in befriending abortionists than in saving babies.

On the interior ground, he will struggle against his own temptations to wrath and hatred. He will struggle against the pride of the lonely righteous man. He will struggle to love his enemies. In a supreme act of self-abasement, he will ask forgiveness from an abortionist for some wrong he has done. The abortionist, instead of being touched, will respond with scorn. The priest will be miserable, but he will persist, unable to deny his calling.

And finally, I picture him dying while saving the abortionist from a zealot's bullet, finally saving a life, though not an unborn life. As the curtain falls, the abortionist stands wondering over his body, and hope is borne aloft.

ʂ̃ʅ̃ ʂ̃ʅ̃ ʂ̃ʅ̃

flannery o'connor and the two-by-four

JESUS DIDN'T HAVE TO BE CRUCIFIED. He didn't have to be scourged. He didn't have to be crowned with thorns. To accomplish the redemption of mankind, all He had to do was suffer the ultimate violence—death. Death was the penalty placed upon Adam and Eve for their sin, the sin in which every soul ever after has mysteriously participated. Christ, the God-man, took that penalty upon Himself, and because He was innocent, His death sufficed to erase the otherwise unpayable debt man owed to God. Then, because He was also God, He was able to conquer death and draw all humanity to Himself. As Paul says, in Adam, all sin; in Christ, all may be raised up as adopted sons of God.

Death is the ultimate violence, but because it is common and sometimes quiet, we may overlook that violence. We talk of dying peacefully. But soul is sundered from body—what's peaceful about that?

Jesus could have died a happy old man, and that would have sufficed for our redemption. But He didn't die a happy old man: He was scourged, crowned with thorns, and cruci-fied. Before that ultimate violence of death, there was lots of preparatory violence. His death was *obviously* violent, obviously unnatural, and very public. There is fittingness to this, but not necessity. Part of that fittingness has to do with manifestation. Jesus' death was meant to be proclaimed to all the world, so that His resurrection might also be proclaimed.

ON FEBRUARY 28 OF 2004, the *New York Times* published an essay by the novelist Mary Gordon that was critical of Mel Gibson's movie *The Passion of the Christ* ("For One Catholic, 'Passion'

Skews the Meaning of the Crucifixion," *The New York Times*, Saturday, 28 February 2004, Arts & Ideas/Cultural Desk). One of Gordon's criticisms concerned the bloody, protracted scourging scene. "A great deal of screen time is taken up with the flagellation of Jesus," she wrote. "What does this accomplish in an understanding of the meaning of Jesus' life and death? How is Jesus different from any other victim of torture?"

I thought Gibson answered this question at the very beginning of the film, in white letters against a black screen: "By his stripes we were healed." I guessed that Gibson dwelt on the scourging because he regarded the lash wounds as visceral manifestations of our sins. Does the beating go on so long as to beggar belief? So does humanity's persistence in sin. I'm not defending Gibson here so much as I'm saying he gave a reason for what he did.

Gordon also asked the film's coscreenwriter (with Gibson), Benedict Fitzgerald, why he made the film so violent. Fitzgerald replied that in an age of violence, you had to use violence to make your point. He then related "a story that had been dear to both his mother," Sally Fitzgerald, and to his mother's friend, Flannery O'Connor. The story was about a man who buys a mule and is told it will do anything if treated with loving kindness. But sugar and the best feed don't get the mule going, and the man takes the mule back. The original owner hits the mule over the head with a two-by-four. "The buyer says, 'But you said he needed to be treated with loving kindness.' The seller says, 'Yes, but you have to get his attention first.'"

So the cowriter of *The Passion* was born to one of Flannery O'Connor's closest friends. Flannery O'Connor, the southern Catholic writer who is regularly linked with the word *grotesque* because of the freakish souls who populate her stories. O'Connor, who wrote in her essay "The Grotesque in Southern Fiction" that the novelist's vision "has to be transmitted and that the limitations and blind spots of his audience will very definitely affect the way in which he is able to show what he sees. This is another thing, which in these times, increases the tendency toward the grotesque in fiction" (*Flannery O'Connor: Collected Works* [New York: The Library of America, 1988], 819).

The reader's need, continued O'Connor, "is to be lifted up. There is something in us . . . that demands the redemptive act, that demands that what falls at least be offered the chance to be restored. The reader of today looks for this motion, and rightly so, but what he has forgotten is the cost of it. His sense of evil is diluted or lacking altogether and so he has forgotten the price of restoration." Gibson and Fitzgerald may not be a match for O'Connor when it comes to artistic mastery, but when I read of the connection between O'Connor and Fitzgerald, I felt I understood the film a little better.

Gordon wrote that, watching *The Passion*, she felt as if she were being continually hit over the head with a two-by-four. Returning to the story of the mule, she complained, "But I never tasted the sugar, and I wasn't even given my portion of healthy feed. Once my attention was grabbed, what was it I was supposed to hear? That Jesus suffered greatly for my sins, more greatly perhaps than I should imagine. But who is this Jesus, and what is the meaning of his suffering?"

"Psychologically," she opined, "the power of the Passion is that it acknowledges the place of suffering, particularly unjust suffering, in human life." I disagree. I think the psychological power of the Passion is that it reveals the gravity of our offense against God when we sin, and the love God showed in redeeming us from that offense. I think that's the message that *The Passion of the Christ* wields like a two-by-four.

ᴥᴥᴥᴥᴥ

O'CONNOR WAS HERSELF ACCUSED of swinging too much heavy lumber, as Paul Elie notes in his book *The Life You Save May Be Your Own: An American Pilgrimage* (New York: Farrar, Straus & Giroux, 2003, 308). Elie reports that when Orville Prescott reviewed O'Connor's *The Violent Bear It Away* for the *New York Times*, he called her characters "caricatured types of human misery . . . one can't believe in them, or care about them."

I first read O'Connor because one of my college tutors said she was a finer fiction writer than Walker Percy. I was still infatuated with Percy, and resented the suggestion that my beloved was not the *ne plus ultra*. But my tutor was a smart, literate man, so I sat down and read O'Connor's short story "A Good Man Is Hard to Find." First I was horrified; then I was flummoxed. *What's going on here? What's all this wretchedness about? This is a great Catholic writer?* I became convinced I just didn't understand literature.

I learned a little in the years that followed. I read O'Connor's *Wise Blood*, and I began to understand what was going on, but I was careful about recommending her. I still am, and here is why. While I was living in my first house, my friend Jake and I attempted to form a Catholic reading group. Jake invited a retired high school Latin teacher to join us. One evening, while my brother, Mark, was visiting, our little group began discussing the question, "What is Catholic literature?" To the Latin teacher, a very decent and no doubt intelligent man, Catholic literature was edifying literature that dealt with Catholics, for Catholics, by Catholics. Chesterton's *Father Brown* and such.

My brother disagreed with passion but not rudeness. He pointed to O'Connor's "A Good Man Is Hard to Find," in particular, to the Misfit's eulogy for the grandmother: "She would of been a good woman if it had been somebody there to shoot her every minute of her life" (*Flannery O'Connor: Collected Works* [New York: The Library of America, 1988], 153). "See?" said my brother. "Only when she was facing death—only in death—could she die to herself. That's what she needed—to die. That was grace for her." The Latin teacher wasn't buying.

I was irritated; I decided to force the issue. I went and fetched Walker Percy's *Lancelot*, a dark book full of dark sentiments. I read a passage that was sexually frank, to put it mildly. It addressed religious matters, and it made sense in context, but what I did was simply crude and offensive. My reading it was a challenge, pure and simple. Can you take it? Can you take this Catholic literature? The Latin teacher, God bless him, did not wither under the blast of obscenity. "I don't see anything Catholic about that," he replied.

Looking back, I admire him for not backing down in the face of my assault. Even a two-by-four requires artful use, and I was pounding away like a lump-headed troglodyte. But I'm not saying I was entirely mistaken; I'm not saying that *Lancelot* isn't Catholic literature—even if it's far from the best example. O'Connor described the Catholic novel as a novel by a Catholic mind looking at anything, and I think it a fine definition. If anything, I would broaden it to include any novel that presents a world the Catholic mind can recognize as true.

Martin Amis is not a Catholic. But I wish I had read his novel *The Information* before our little group's discussion that evening.

"Look here," I would have begun. "At first blush, it might look as if *The Information* is positively anti-Catholic. One character (who isn't Catholic) feels driven to cheat on his wife (who is) because she won't fellate him and won't use birth control. The strictures of her faith are a great big wedge in their marriage. The book's hero accuses a decaying Catholic patriarch of having 'a gamekeeper God.'

"Ah, but look what happens," I would have said. "First, Amis takes Christ's line about gaining the world and losing your soul and gives it a name: Gwyn Barry. The guy writes a book that makes him a fabulously wealthy international superstar. He marries a Lady, a gorgeous Roman Catholic, as it happens. Everything is great, but really, it's not. He spirals into himself in grand fashion. And he becomes jealous of the wretched Richard Tull. So jealous that he employs trainers to finally be able to beat Tull at tennis, at snooker, at chess. So jealous that he turns Tull's wife Gina into his whore."

And then, the kicker. "Why is he jealous of Tull? Because Tull has love. Tull loves his wife and kids, however poorly, and they love him. Why does Barry make Gina his whore? Because there's something real in Tull's marriage, and Barry wants to defile it.

"And there at the end, can you imagine a scene of purer grace? Tull has finally been stripped of everything. Gwyn Barry wins, except he doesn't. The one source of love in his life has dried up. Tull, on the other hand, knows that if he can forgive Gina her infidelity, then she will never leave him—he won't lose love."

Finally, "When the wind sweeps down the street and fills the air with apple blossoms as Tull weeps with joy, can the movement be anything other than the Holy Spirit? The last paragraph is purest nihilism, but that's just the author talking. The world he shows us is true. *That's* what I mean by a Catholic novel."

That would have been better. But I hadn't read *The Information*, and besides, I was full of zeal. I had forgotten my own first reaction to O'Connor's Misfit.

I WAS REMINDED OF THAT ZEAL at a wedding a couple of years ago. Somebody introduced me to someone he knew—"He's into Catholic literature, like you." Oh, dread . . . I hardly read enough to qualify as being "into" much of anything, though the few books I do own and reread tend to run to Catholics: O'Connor, Evelyn Waugh, J. F. Powers, Walker Percy, etc. So there I was with this fellow, and right away, he was down on Willa Cather, *Death Comes for the Archbishop*, and pious

Catholic readers who couldn't take anything "stronger," like O'Connor. I was pained by this reminder of my old opinion. I said I needed to fill my glass, which was true, and did not return to the conversation.

Whence comes this anger, this desire to force open the eyes of fellow Catholics? It is as if one were scandalized by someone else's being scandalized. "What? You think this is offensive? You think it's not edifying? Don't you know we Catholics have to be able to look life—with all its ugliness, horror, evil, and offensiveness—full in the face and still affirm God's providence? Otherwise, it's all just a happy dream!" All this is true. And happily, we have Christ's help in this, since he gives meaning to all that suffering and horror. But that doesn't mean everybody's got to be able to read O'Connor.

In her essay, "The Church and the Fiction Writer," O'Connor writes that "Catholic readers are constantly being offended and scandalized by novels that they don't have the fundamental equipment to read in the first place, and often these are works that are permeated with a Christian spirit" (*Flannery O'Connor: Collected Works* [New York: The Library of America, 1988], 811). "Aha!" says the "strong" reader, the one who can take the hard stuff.

But she also writes that "what leads the writer to his salvation may lead the reader into sin. . . . The business of protecting souls from dangerous literature belongs properly to the Church. All fiction, even when it satisfies the requirements of art, will not turn out to be suitable for everyone's consumption. . . ." (ibid., 810). O'Connor took this claim seriously, applying to her bishop for permission before reading books that had been placed on the Index. At this, even the "strong" reader would do well to pause and temper his zeal.

I think of my mother, who never liked short stories because they are almost always sad. This from a woman with her master's in English literature. I cannot dismiss her—she's Mom—so I have to consider her position. I know she knows suffering, and that she does not shy away from it. I have watched her lose friends to differences over abortion, seen her pour herself out in the care of her parents and her in-laws. I know she is sad that I live so far away.

But her maxim of "Whatever God wants" is aimed at her own soul as well as mine. She accepts sadness. Perhaps the fictional sadness she shies away from is rather fictional despair. Despair is common enough in fiction, and not without reason. And there is certainly value in its presentation. But thanks to

Mom, I have a little more tolerance for those who choose not to read about it, and who dwell on hope instead.

ℐℐℐℐℐ

the light under the bushel

DISTANCES, SOMETIMES EVEN SHORT ONES, take their toll on friendships. After I moved to La Mesa, I saw a lot less of my friend Jake. Our Catholic book club didn't last. Now, when we cross paths, we say we'll have to get together, and once or twice, it's actually happened. But most of the time, something comes up.

It eats at me a little. When we met, Jake was a recent convert to the faith, in large part through his reading. George Macdonald led to C. S. Lewis, and Lewis led to Chesterton, and Chesterton to the church. Jake was single and middle-aged, and I don't think he had much in the way of a community of faith. He liked being around us, and we liked him. Now that I don't see him, I sometimes worry. His newfound faith was already hitting some rough patches back when we saw each other more often. He would miss Mass for a few weeks, start drifting. *How's he doing now? What if he's faltering again?*

The last time he faltered, I wondered if the problem was joy—or rather, its lack. Jake told me that joy was what attracted him to Christianity. I thought this both odd and fascinating; I had never given much thought to joy. I thought joy was only for mature souls, souls that could follow James's counsel to "count it all joy" (James 1:2) and rejoice even in the midst of suffering. I still tend to ask for deliverance instead of giving thanks, or at best, I offer grim acceptance. I can sometimes manage fidelity. Perseverance—yes, that. Occasionally, maybe even love. But I don't look for joy. I don't really know what it is.

I wondered if Jake understood joy. I wondered if he had come to the faith looking for joy, and found the elation of a soul newly incorporated into the Mystical Body of Christ. I wondered if that elation had faded with time, and if that was the root of his trouble.

I began to understand his idea of the Christian life as essentially joyful when I read C. S. Lewis's *The Great Divorce*. Wielding a bit of theological license, Lewis describes a meeting of the residents of heaven and hell on a somewhat neutral middle ground. The saints are attempting to convince the damned to follow them to heaven. Nearly all of the damned are certain they are happier in hell than they could ever be in paradise. In hell, they get to hold onto their sinful, sorry selves: their cherished prejudices, their petty grudges. Over and over, Lewis stresses the *joy* of heaven—the delight in entering its bright reality—over the misery of hell and its illusory satisfactions. He describes a saint from whom "the invitation to all joy" is "singing out of her whole being like a bird's song on an April evening." The song, says Lewis the observer, "seemed to me such that no creature could resist it" (*The Best of C. S. Lewis* [New York: The Iverson Associates, 1969], 183).

Another saint gave a speech that pricked my conscience. "There have been men before now who got so interested in proving the existence of God that they came to care nothing for God Himself. . . . there have been some who were so occupied in spreading Christianity that they never gave a thought to Christ" (ibid., 156). Or those who gave so much thought to a friend's crisis of faith that they forgot to pray for him. I said a Hail Mary, and asked God to bring Jake back.

ꙮꙮꙮꙮꙮ

JAKE'S CRISIS OF FAITH helped me to recognize another persistent sin of omission on my part: the failure to treat people as fellow members of Christ's body, and instead, to regard them from a safe distance. There's a little laziness in this, and a dollop of trepidation, but it's largely a failing of charity. Most of

the time, I can get away with it, because Deirdre is so wonderfully social. People confide in her, seek her out in times of
trouble. (Tom had told *her* about his woes, not me.) She tells
me their troubles, and I offer counsel. So it works out—I help
Deirdre to help others. But it keeps me at arm's length, and
that's a danger. It keeps me from really encountering other
people. I believe, but I'm a pretty lousy face-to-face witness.

During college, I visited my high school buddy Steven at
his university. An atheist—or at least a person who did not
believe in anything like a personal God—he had taken up with
a bunch of bluff, good-natured Catholics who had attended
Catholic high school in Chicago. My immediate impression
of them was that they dragged themselves to Mass on Sunday
but did not let being Catholic interfere with having as good a
time as they pleased come Saturday night. Steven told me he
suspected that he knew more about the faith than they did. My
response—thought of weeks later, and never given voice—was
that, however little they knew, they knew that what they knew
was true. I thought that was no small difference, even if it didn't
seem to be having much effect at the time. Life is long.

I once proposed to begin a correspondence with Steven
regarding my faith, and he agreed to participate. But when
I sat down to write the opening salvo, I found I didn't have
the heart for it. It would have been just that—a salvo, a strike

against his unbelief. I think I sensed that I wasn't about to convert him through debate. I wasn't sure I was smart enough, and even if I was, I wasn't sure anybody would ever convert through argument. My brother's friend Chip had read his way into the church, principally through Augustine, but it was Mark's model of the Christian life that laid the groundwork. Mark had been a friend to Chip, and Chip had seen that Christianity was not some airy theory. I hadn't really spoken with Steven in over a year.

I once picked up a "How to Evangelize" pamphlet at a youth retreat. Step One was, "Make a friend." Then it was on to Step Two and the various ways you could set about inviting your friend to consider the faith. When Mark saw the pamphlet, and saw the three little words of Step One all but swamped by what followed, he laughed. He said that "Make a friend" was easily the most important step, however forlorn it appeared. But at least they had put it first.

I DON'T HAVE MANY FRIENDS, and most of the ones I do have are Catholic. But there is one, David, who is not Catholic. He may be an unbeliever.

How can I not be certain? How can this man whom I grace with the name "friend" have a spiritual life that is unknown to me? Part of it has to do with his mode of relating. More than anyone I know, he continually asks questions—about me. He doesn't hide behind them—he answers my reciprocal queries readily enough—but his curiosity seems limitless. He has a gift for getting me to talk. He is an excellent listener; part of the reason I blather so is that I feel I have in him an interested ear. I tell him of my struggles against Satan, of my efforts at prayer and penance, of saints' interventions and signs of God's providence. I have no idea what he thinks of all this. While I sometimes hope that it serves as a kind of witness, I'm not trying to impress him; and I have never spoken with an eye toward convincing him of the faith. I'm just telling him about my life.

David attended Thomas Aquinas College. We were not particularly close then. But then he married Claire—a Catholic and a great friend to Deirdre—and that proved the occasion for our friendship. One of his wedding party failed to show up; I stepped in. I listened to him promise to accept children willingly from God, and to raise them in the faith of the church. Later, I became godfather to his first child. When our families get together, he almost always joins us at Mass.

He has kept the promises that he made at the altar, but his interior life is still a mystery to me. He knows the church; he loves its members; he obeys its moral teaching. I sometimes wonder if he feels a desire to avoid being converted by simple proximity. A soul might be loath to be absorbed as if by an amoeba. But I don't know if he feels that way. And of course, faith is not reason. Faith is a gift. Augustine argued that even the desire to pray for the gift of faith is itself a gift. It's not an excuse to just sit back and watch God work, but it is something to remember.

I feel such a commonality with David; it is easy not to think of this distance between us. But it is there. I did not make a friend in order to win a convert, and it's not as if I feel obliged to win him over. That's God's affair. And when I am with him, I do not feel the weight of things unsaid. It's only when we're apart that I wonder if I should feel uncomfortable about not mentioning the elephant in the room.

ℬℬℬℬℬ

WHY SHOULD I BE EMBARRASSED? Why, after I say grace before meals in public places, do I brace myself for the question, "Are you a Catholic?" Sometimes it comes, sometimes it doesn't. But when I answer yes, that is almost always the end of it. Certainly, no one has ever attacked me for it. So why the embarrassment?

I got my answer when I read the *Publishers Weekly* review of Garry Wills's book, *Why I Am a Catholic*. Particularly, the sentence that read, "He has remained Catholic, he says, because his faith is based on 'the great truths of salvation,' found in the creed, which he believes Catholicism has played a major role in preserving" ("Forecasts," *Publishers Weekly* 249, no. 25 [July 1, 2002]). Like Wills, I think the great truths of salvation *are* found in the Creed. But if you asked me why I am a Catholic, my first answer would be the Eucharist—I want that communion with God. I need it.

You see the difference? Wills opts for a profession of faith; I go for a personal encounter. I am not criticizing Wills here. If anything, the Creed makes for a better witness; it's more like something you can share with another. Though I love what is universal and communicable about the faith, my sense of my own faith is deeply personal. It's intimate, almost like sex is intimate. I am not ashamed to be Catholic, but I have a hard time proclaiming it.

CHRISTMAS OF 2000 brought me back to Cortland, and as I drove around the snowy streets, I was struck by the number of Marian statues in people's front yards, proclaiming the household's Catholicism to every passerby. I had grown up seeing them, but now I took more notice. Since arriving in California, I have heard stories of odd beliefs and practices. If you make a request of St. Joseph and he is slow to answer it, you can expedite matters if you bury a statue of him upside down. Sometimes, folks will steal the statue from a church, holding the saint hostage until their demands are met.

I smile when I imagine the scene in the confessional: "Father, I'm the one who stole St. Joseph. I needed a new roof . . . and . . . I buried him upside down. But the loan came through, so I'm bringing him back." But I never heard of such practices in Cortland. I imagine people looked on their statues as material reminders of an immaterial world, and as wholesome décor besides.

I don't remember many statues in our home growing up. (Today is a different story.) My first memorable experience with a statue came during my visit to Assisi. While visiting St. Francis's basilica, our tour group was shown a statue of Francis adjacent to the cloister walk. The stone statue held a stone birds' nest, but the bird in the nest, though motionless, was alive. After a while, another bird alighted on the nest's edge, and the two switched places like sentries at a post. The guide informed us that the nest was never empty, that one bird always replaced another. As miracles go, it almost seemed silly, but there it was, gaining value from its superfluity.

Then, while I was in college, my parents placed a white concrete statue of Mary in our living room and began saying their rosary in front of it. At the beginning of the rosary, they would offer prayers for our Lady's intentions at Medjugorje. As the months went by, the statue acquired a heavy dusting of gold flecks, concentrated in the folds of her robe and about her face; the flecks remain to this day. This is no proof of the Medjugorje apparition, but it is extraordinary. Even if it is the work of some demon seeking to lead souls astray, it is rather shocking evidence of the supernatural—shocking because it happened in my childhood home. "This is the living room where I scarfed buffalo wings and watched college basketball. What's God doing in here?"

Then there are events that look miraculous only to those who have eyes to see. I think of the climbing rose in the yard behind our own, a rose that wound its way over the fence and cascaded down around my mother's Marian shrine, surrounding our Lady with a nimbus of yellow blooms. Our neighbor cut the rose back hard in an effort to retrain it; she wanted the plant to aim its bounty toward her. It never quite grew back.

Still, our statues were of the backyard or indoor variety. Our devotion was not so public as the front-yarders, or as that of an acquaintance who harvested a life-size Mary and Joseph from a renovated church and set them up in her dining room. So I was uneasy when my wife suggested a saint's statue for the front yard of our second house. I wanted roses for the yard's centerpiece, and then my wife thought of a trellis, and under the trellis . . . St. Thérèse of Lisieux, the great giver of roses.

I hesitated. Was it too public, too aggressive? We were the only churchgoing Catholics on our cul-de-sac. There were a couple of lapsed Catholics—would they see it as an accusation?

Would they think we were proclaiming our piety? Was I hesitating out of stupid pride, secretly ashamed to be associated with the superstitious (people who, while superstitious, might be far holier than me)?

I was not at all comfortable with the idea, and then I was. I suppose there is no explanation for it, other than grace. I started looking for a St. Thérèse statue. I didn't find one I liked, but while shopping for roses at Hunter's Nursery in Lemon Grove, I came across a St. Joseph that seemed perfect. I bought him almost on impulse, and set him up under the trellis in a pounding rain as soon as we got home. Suddenly, it was obvious—time and again during the buying and refinancing and remodeling and relandscaping of our home, we had offered prayers to St. Joseph that all would go well, and all *had* gone well. And suddenly, there I was, right back with my upstate forebears and their prominent statues.

I have no idea how my little shrine was received. People praised the front yard and the roses, but no one mentioned the statue. The only possible clue: During a discussion of the Christian church that several of my neighbors attended, someone joked to my wife about the possibility of my "converting." "Oh, no," chortled another neighbor, "he's Catholic all the way."

᧨᧨᧨᧨᧨

THE STATUE WITNESSED TO MY FAITH without any further help from me. As I said, I don't see much of Jake, though that's not really an excuse. With David, I feel like the moment will present itself. But family is different. With family, I get a sense of urgency, as if we're too close for this difference to exist without causing damage. My mother-in-law is a lapsed Catholic from way back. She has told me that the faith just never took hold in her. Deirdre says her mom had bad experiences with the nuns who taught her in school. I have heard of a wedding she was not allowed to attend, because the Catholic bride was marrying outside the church.

"Lapsed" might be too passive a word for Mom. She is not a passive person. A former president of the Kansas City chapter of NOW, she is ardently pro-choice and quite pagan in her spirituality.

Whatever I think of her spirituality or politics, I know Mom has many virtues. She recently retired from a career as a public health nurse, a job that involved loving service to the poor. She loves Deirdre despite their differences, and she loves her grandchildren. Every time we have a baby, she flies out from Kansas City and helps us get through life while Deirdre recovers.

It was after the birth of Olivia, our third, that Mom didn't attend Mass with us. There was a practical reason. There wasn't room in our car for three kids (two in car seats) and three adults. But we couldn't say that to Fin; it wouldn't wash. This was Mass, which he knew we were obliged to attend. "Grandma goes to a different church," explained my wife when Fin asked where she was. Fin took the statement at face value. I was grateful. I didn't want to explain that the "church" she was referring to was a group of women gathered at the altar in Grandma's home for goddess worship. (Grandma is sympathetic to our discomfort; when we visit, she puts the altar out of sight. I am grateful.)

Mom told us about one such ritual later that day—a celebration of Passover that "incorporated elements from Christianity, Judaism, and feminist spirituality." She and her friends likened "the oppression of women by the patriarchy" to the Israelites' slavery in Egypt.

"What do you mean by 'oppression'?" asked Deirdre.

"Well, for example, women not being able to be priests," she replied. "I have several friends who are nuns who wish they could do that."

I knew my wife was wondering if I would jump into the fray and offer some account of the all-male priesthood. But how? A simple appeal to history—Christ commanded only the twelve male apostles to "Do this in remembrance of me"—would not avail; she was no great believer in history, as I had learned a while back. She and her friends once celebrated a kind of anti–St. Patrick's Day, having decided that the snakes he supposedly drove out of Ireland were not snakes at all, but witches—her spiritual forebears. I pointed out that as a missionary, Patrick was not in a position to drive witches or anybody else out of Ireland, and that his life was spent *converting* pagans, not driving them away. "We just decided that that's what it meant," she replied, unfazed.

An appeal to the ontological distinction between male and female, such as the one given by St. Thomas when he explains why we call God "Father," would just smack of the patriarchy she had mentioned. Further, she treats philosophy much the same way she treats history. My wife once drove her all the way to the brink of admitting that, in her judgment, the mother's will determined the status of the fetus. By her account, my wife's fetuses were all "babies" because they were wanted, but other, unwanted fetuses lacked personhood. I kept silent on the question of women priests; my mother-in-law is not going to be won back to the faith through argument.

I think God haunts Mom. She once told me that she never really had faith. But when Deirdre's brother didn't have his firstborn baptized right away, she became agitated. "Why do you care, Mom?" asked Deirdre. "You don't believe any of it."

"I just think it's important."

Why does she think it's important? I don't think it's because of any witness. Some Catholics she knows are no better as persons (certainly no happier) than anybody else. And while Mom tells us she's grateful that Deirdre and I have a good marriage, we don't exactly "sing out the invitation to all joy." We're hesitant to bring up anything divisive—we see so little of her; Mom is sacrificing to be out here; she is a great help. And when she visits, we have trouble maintaining the normal course of our own relationship. The chasm between Mom and us is before us always. It's more than differing theology; it's a different sense of life. Sometimes, Deirdre isn't sure what to say to Mom about anything, and it makes Deirdre sadder than I've ever seen her.

When something like abortion does come up, Deirdre tends to lose control of her emotions. She once threatened not to tell Mom when she was pregnant, since it wasn't really a baby until it was born. Mom was hurt. Deirdre was ashamed.

It's gotten better of late, especially when we pray in preparation for the visit. Deirdre and her mother have had some peaceful exchanges about abortion: Mom said that working with developmentally disabled children during the last years of her nursing career helped change her mind about whether their life was worth living. Deirdre introduced Mom to Justice For

All, a pro-life campus crusade, and Mom responded positively. But we're still frustrated.

Once, after Mom left, I talked to Ernie about our distress. Here was such a clear call for evangelization within our own family, and we felt paralyzed and impotent. "Yes," he replied, "I've been frustrated with the lack of formal prayer in our family as well."

At first, I thought it a bizarre statement. Had Ernie been distracted? Mom needs a stirring in her heart, not rites and rituals. But maybe Ernie was on to something. Rites and rituals give structure to the religious dimension of life. If we weren't always at our best when Mom arrived, how much more important that we have that structure to support us? And in daily Mass or the rosary, we wouldn't be just obeying the institutional commands, we would be seeking after something personal. And finally, if we practiced those devotions, if we worked harder on attaining personal holiness, perhaps we would find a way to share it with her.

I want Mom to see something attractive in the faith, something she wants and does not have. I want her to see in our lives evidence that ours is a living God, one who acts in the human heart in a way the goddess does not. I have said that I do not seek experience of God. But experience may be just what Mom needs.

≋≋≋≋≋

THERE ARE MANY WAYS TO WITNESS. My father is a great believer in conversion stories. He sends people excerpts from Fr. John O'Brien's four-volume collection *The Road to Damascus* to people. At least two of them have subsequently entered the church. He writes letters to his unbelieving brother, content to remain silent on the matter when they meet. But sometimes, the opportunity—the obligation—literally comes knocking on your door.

Elena was at Thomas Aquinas College for a while and became friends with Deirdre. Elena had been through a lot. As a teenager, she ran away from an abusive father. She became a rich man's mistress. He abandoned her in New York City; his driver gave her some money, dropped her off, and told her not to come back.

After college, she kept in sporadic contact with Deirdre. Sometimes, we would go years between phone calls. But in October 2004, she came to stay with us for a few weeks. She was in bad shape. She'd been through a breakdown and was convinced that the government was watching her because of some e-mails she'd sent after 9/11. Odd coincidences resonated with terrible meaning. She saw fresh evidence of her peril everywhere she looked.

Medication helped some—her aunt sent her some anti-depressants—and she was able to find a job and an apartment in San Diego. I had tried to be helpful once or twice, but as usual, it was Deirdre who did most of the consoling. It was Deirdre who encouraged Elena to join us at Mass, to return to her exploration of the faith. (Elena had recently gotten involved with spell-casting.) But when Elena came walking down the driveway one afternoon while Deirdre was away, I knew there was a problem, and I knew I would have to deal with it.

The fear was back on her. I expressed sympathy, asked what I could do. She asked for a drink, and I made her a gin and tonic. We stood in the kitchen.

"I'm just so scared, Matthew."

"Look, Elena, it's like I said before. Even if the danger is real, there isn't anything you can do about it. What you can do is pray for peace, so that you're not gripped by terror. You can put yourself under the Blessed Mother's protection. No matter what happens, you can ask for the grace to accept it. Would you like to say a decade of the rosary?"

"Sure. Okay."

And so we prayed together—me leading, she responding. She finished her drink, thanked me, and went back to her job. It was the best I had ever done.

ɹᴑɹᴑɹᴑɹᴑɹᴑ

the best thing in the world

DEIRDRE AND I WERE VISITING CLAIRE in her new home while her husband was away on business. It was a Saturday morning, full of Southern California sunshine. We had just finished breakfast; later, there would be a birthday party for Claire's daughter.

Into the midst of all this bright pleasantness came Claire's rather dark confession. She had found herself taking a certain delight in the news that John Geoghan—the defrocked priest whose sexual abuse of boys ignited the current scandal—had been strangled in his prison cell. She suspected her delight was less than perfectly Christian, but said she was still hesitant to suppress it. She wanted to know what we thought.

It wasn't a new scenario. Claire is not docile by temperament, but she tries to rein herself in. She is not afraid to be wrong, or even to appear foolish, and that makes her honest and forthright. When she doesn't understand or disagrees with church teaching, she talks to someone who does understand, or at least someone who _does_ agree and is willing to seek understanding. Sometimes, that someone is me. She does not easily give in, but she will consider what she hears long after a conversation has ended. I admire her spirit, and I do my best to play defender of the faith to my fellow Catholic.

My brain latched onto a line I thought I remembered from Scripture: "God does not delight in the death of his enemies. Rather, He rejoices at the repentance of sinners." I clung to the line, almost shamefacedly—surely I could do better? I warned against confusing bloodlust with justice. She came back with the Old Testament, where blood and justice were more frequently linked. "I think if it were more like that, we'd value life more. We don't value life enough."

I said the New Testament represented a break from the Old with regard to vengeance—viz. turning the other cheek, loving your enemies, etc. I argued for mercy, but secretly, I felt squishy. I know that I am softhearted. Mercy is not softheartedness. Mercy is not squeamishness with regard to justice. Mercy is not weakness, but one may be weak and call it mercy.

Claire hung on. This wasn't a man killing another man or raping a woman. This was a *priest*, destroying the lives of *boys*. That he was a priest made all the difference to Claire. "How can people who are so close to the sacraments be this way? It makes me wonder about the sacraments." She was scandalized where I was not, but I understood her reaction. I think to myself that I am not shaken by the sins of men, even men who are consecrated to God. But she was looking at what they do. These were men who changed bread and wine to Body and Blood every day, men who acted *in persona Christi* to forgive the sins of others. How could men who did these holy things also do these monstrous things? It can be hard to think of priests as mere men, sinners like the rest of us. It is even harder to think of them as mere conduits of grace, as unaffected by the daily miracles they perform as a power line is unaffected by the electricity it conducts.

We went 'round and 'round until we were repeating ourselves. Silence settled in; I kept washing dishes. A few minutes later, Claire said, "I'm probably having this reaction because of my own frustration. I pray and pray and try and try and nothing changes. I pray for conversions, and nothing happens. It makes me wonder. And then this happens." As usual, I was impressed by her humility and honesty, her willingness to lay out her inner workings.

Deirdre stepped in. "The smallest act of love has merit. Think of Thérèse's Little Way."

Claire was unmoved. "Yes, but Thérèse prayed for the conversion of a murderer when she was five years old, and the murderer converted. That's not small. She knew going in."

I OFTEN FEEL SIMILAR FRUSTRATION. In *Amadeus*, the conductor Salieri was able to recognize genius, but he didn't possess it, and the difference tormented him. So it is with me and holiness. Listening to my parents—who are so much further along that holy road—I sometimes feel as if they are speaking to me from another world, trying desperately to use words I'll understand. Love the cross. Love failure. Give thanks for frustration. Love the cross.

I've been reading Ron Hansen's novel *Mariette in Ecstasy* (New York: Edward Burlingame Books, 1991) out loud to Deirdre. In it, a nun reads to her fellow sisters that St. John of the Cross, when asked by Jesus to choose some gift for himself, requested "naught but suffering and to be despised for your sake." Maybe it's not another world my parents are speaking from; maybe they've just crossed a bridge, one crossed by so many saints before them. St. Pio: "If we knew the value of suffering, we would ask for more." St. John Vianney: "I used to have a fear of crosses, until I prayed for the love of crosses." Suffering must still be suffering to these people, but if it is their heart's desire, it must also be overlaid with sweetness. Suffering conforms them to Christ, helps them to forget themselves and think only of Him. Suffering helps them to love, and so they love suffering. I can say the words, but it's still too much for me to make them mean anything to my own will.

Love. Father Harry Neely, an Augustinian priest here in San Diego, once said to me in conversation, "I know God is my lover." When he said it, he was stating a fact. He was not fishing for the spark of interest that may come from speaking of God in such intimate terms. But I felt the spark anyway.

The word *love* has been emptied out, watered down, twisted and generally misused to the point where its association with true charity seems forced, inauthentic. I feel uncomfortable using it in an unsentimental, religious context. I feel like I'm the one doing the twisting, the misusing.

But it's precisely love that will drag me out of my timidity about my Catholicism. And I am timid. I never hesitate to admit that I am a Catholic, but the fact that I feel as if I am admitting it is problem enough. I am not bold; I do not boast in the Lord. I fear I am most comfortable regarding myself as the member of a particularly enlightened sect, a thought that runs contrary to the very name of my faith—catholic, universal. I envy my brother, who is at ease with the claim that the Catholic Church sees the world as it really is, that our view is true and universal and coherent. Mark can argue with confidence that it is the world that is mistaken.

"I know God is my lover"—what a beautiful thing to be able to say. But also terrible. God the lover can and will demand that I give Him everything, even my precious will. He promises that He will lead me to find myself, but only after I lose myself in Him. How often do the saints express their longing to be nothing, so that God may be all? I don't want to be nothing. I cannot imagine God being all.

"Peace" has suffered just as "love." When I hear peace spoken of, I almost always think, "Thou criest 'Peace, peace,' but there is no peace." (I'm not even certain that's in the Bible; I heard Orson Welles say it on the *Begatting of the President* record album. Orson Welles sounds a little like God, so it sits in my memory as scripture.) The angels at the Nativity proclaimed, "Peace on earth," but they directed their proclamation "to men of goodwill." Christ came to bring the peace of God, to heal a division between God and man. But he left behind a Church Militant; the world's peace is not the peace of God. C. S. Lewis wrote, "There is no neutral ground in the universe; every square inch, every split second, is claimed by God and counterclaimed by Satan" (C. S. Lewis, *Christian Reflections* [Grand Rapids: William B. Eerdmans, 1967], 33). A spiritual war is raging within me and within the soul of every person, no matter how peaceful things look on the outside.

It's easy to forget this war even exists. I long for leadership, for the general's rallying cry. *I need* is the name of the enemy in all his particular forms, his tactics, his weapons, his weaknesses. I need help.

Too often, I look for that help from the pulpit. When it doesn't come—or worse, when what *does* come disturbs the little peace I have—I feel bitter. Where is my pastor? Where is my shepherd? I don't want him to sanctify my soul for me. I do want his support and guidance.

I was so happy when San Diego's Bishop Brom requested that his Holy Year Proclamation be read in every parish in the diocese at the beginning of the 2003 Liturgical Year. He opened with a forthright statement of fact—"Left to ourselves, we are helpless before the powers of darkness and death, sin and evil." Then he went on to claim union with Jesus as the answer to this problem, and to hold up "the traditional pillars of spirituality"—prayer, penance, and works of charity—as "the way to encounter Christ . . . and to live in communion with him." He suggested that families pray the rosary and perform acts of charity weekly during the Holy Year, that people go to confession, and that Fridays involve some kind of fasting.

Union with Jesus. God is my lover. The smallest act of love has merit. One of the quotations at the front of Walker Percy's novel *The Last Gentleman* (New York: Farrar, Straus & Giroux, 1966) is from Romano Guardini's *The End of the Modern World*. It reads in part: "We know now that the modern world is coming to an end. . . . Love will disappear from the face of the public world, but the more precious will be the love that flows from one lonely person to another . . . the world to come will be filled with animosity and danger, but it will be a world open and clean." Many of the old institutions and traditions that mandated charity and called it civility are crumbling. I see bumper stickers that show Calvin peeing on "All y'all," that tell me, "My other ride is your mother."

Just now, we seem to be in an awful middle ground—what Percy called the "Christ-haunted, Christ-forgetting" world in the opening line of *Love in the Ruins*. Some might call it Christ-hungover. He lingers, a painful leftover presence that punishes the conscience but brings no comfort. People are left with the sad thrill of transgression: those enraged bumper stickers, the endless appeals to sex that is "perfectly natural," but still sold as "naughty." Such may be the penalty for knowing His rules without knowing Him.

AS FOR WHAT IS TO COME, the world is indeed increasingly filled with animosity and danger, but it is not yet a world open and clean. Sentiment keeps its hold long after principle has rotted away. I think of this when I hear people call America a "Christian nation." If America were populated entirely by non-Christians, would America cease to be?

I am not immune to sentiment. I resent feeling like I can't send my kids to public school, not so much for what they will (or won't) be taught there, but because I don't want to see my eight-year-old daughter at a school talent show someday, thrusting her hips and lip-synching to Shania Twain about what keeps her warm in the middle of the night. I don't even want her watching other eight-year-olds doing it. I don't want my sons developing contempt for their family and an adoration for being cool before they even hit puberty. I see signs of it already. Already, Finian has told me that when he is a father, he will let his kids decide whether they have to go to church—that's how it is in his friend's house.

But why should I resent it? If other parents are happy to rock out and sing along while their daughters ape pop sexpots, who am I to protest? It's a public school; it reflects public mores.

This country assimilates and homogenizes cultures, both religious and ethnic. In Philip Roth's short story "Eli, The Fanatic," one assimilated Jew speaks to another about a Yeshiva that has just opened in their town full of "modern Jews and Protestants."

> We're not just dealing with people. These are religious
> fanatics is what they are. Dressing like that. What I'd

really like to find out is what goes on up there. . . . It smells like a lot of hocus-pocus abracadabra stuff to me. . . . Look, I don't even know about this Sunday School business. Sundays I drive my oldest kid all the way to Scarsdale to learn Bible stories. . . . and you know what she comes up with? This Abraham in the Bible was going to kill his own kid for a sacrifice. She gets nightmares from it, for God's sake! You call that religion? Today a guy like that they'd lock him up. . . . All the place is, is a hideaway for people who can't face life. (*Goodbye, Columbus: And Five Short Stories* [New York: Vintage Books, 1993], 276–77)

Eating Jesus? Homeschooling families with ten kids? Lighting candles in front of statues, confessing sins to a priest in a box? Fanatics. But we can add "modern Catholics" to the list of "modern Jews and Protestants." Catholics fornicate, get divorced and remarry, contracept, and get abortions—same as everybody else. Opinion polls tell us that a lot of Catholics don't believe in Christ's presence in the Eucharist. If some of us resist assimilation, why should we be surprised when the assimilating world hates us, just as it hated Christ, just as Christ promised?

But here's the thing. We can't hide away and not face life. We can't rely on the public world for support, but we have to love. Somebody wrote in to the magazine *Salon* to discuss her uncertainty about becoming a parent. "What would be the return on the investment?" she asked. Some of the magazine's staff thought the author of the letter "crass" and "emotionally crippled." *Salon* used the letter as the catalyst for a series of articles questioning whether having children is worthwhile.

My mother often says, "Children are the only game in town." I happen to think she's right, but such axioms won't hold up in the new age. People aren't pious enough, not toward Mother, and not toward Mother Church. I say bravo to that uncertain woman. Let's be open and clean. Let's drag this out into the light and discuss. Let's not be shocked and resentful; let's love the lonely. Perhaps, coming from a fanatic, the message of God's love will regain some of its wonderful outrageousness. "Listen. I have a secret. I eat God, and I have His life in me. It's the best thing in the world; it leads to everlasting life. But first, you have to die to yourself."